Showing you
cutting through the

# Be Your Truth

## By Amy Goldberg

Amy Goldberg

BE YOUR TRUTH © Copyright 2019 by Amy Goldberg - All rights reserved. No part of this book may be used or reproduced in any manner whatsoever without written permission except in the case of brief quotations embodied in critical articles and reviews.

www.thetrustrise.com

Be Your Truth

To my mother and father who are somewhere looking over me. Whom am I kidding? They haven't a care in the world. And, yet, how dare they leave me here to contend with life and all its confusion. Truth be told--and, hey, that's what this book is all about-- I don't think I really knew how to be my truth until my parents passed away. It was in my aloneness that I finally started to take a look at how to be in this world, to have the courage to trust my truth.

To my beautiful husband, Tommy, who IS here for me to be my truth. He is the closest person I know that really does understand how to Be Your Truth. He discovered, I'm convinced from a past life, that fear is his friend, not his foe, where he trusts his truth to live his truth. Now that's empowering! And I'm grateful for him.

# Contents

## Introduction

Be Your Truth                                       1

## PART 1: How Did We Get Here?

It Starts With You                                  6
Life As We Know It                                  9
What's In A Name?                                  13
5 Ways To Turn FOMO to JOMO                        16
What's Grounding You?                              20
Change Happens. How Do You Handle It?              24
I Now Know The Secret Of Success                   26
Listen Up! It's Important                          29
Love Made Us Do It                                 32
Ready. Set. Go.                                    37
Stop Kidding Yourself. Culture Matters             40
The Power Of Listening                             45
You Know What You'd Be Great At?                   48
Are You Ready For A Change?                        51
Excuse me?                                         54
Asking The Hard Questions                          58
5 Ways To Take Action                              62
What's It All About?                               67
Boss Is Not Boss (At All)                          70
Why?                                               73

| | |
|---|---|
| Are You Lonesome Tonight? | 76 |
| You Have To Do It To Feel It. | 79 |
| Love | 82 |
| Who Are You? | 84 |
| I Know What's Holding You Back | 88 |
| When Life Disappoints You | 91 |
| People Don't Get You | 94 |
| What's It All About? | 97 |
| Good & Bad Days | 100 |
| Loneliness Is a Lonely Word | 104 |
| The Pivot | 107 |

## PART 2: Is It Just Me?

| | |
|---|---|
| Is It Just Me? | 111 |
| A Real Jerk | 119 |
| Are You Sure You Mean To Say Smart? | 123 |
| But … | 126 |
| Is Motivation Overrated? | 129 |
| Let's Not Use The Word "Let" | 133 |
| Please. Stop. Networking | 136 |
| The WOW Factor | 142 |
| When Motivation Does Not Work | 147 |
| Blah, Blah, Rah, Rah | 150 |
| Just My Luck | 153 |
| Stop Selling; Tag 2 Friends If … | 157 |

| | |
|---|---|
| Emotionally, Speaking | 160 |
| Are You A Person Of Your Word? | 163 |
| You're Not Getting It | 166 |
| How Do You Cut Through The Bullsh*t | 169 |
| Overdeliver Is Something We Say | 171 |
| Walk To The Right? | 175 |
| Keep Telling Yourself That | 179 |
| Neutral Face | 183 |

## PART 3: Be Your Truth

| | |
|---|---|
| Be Your Potential | 186 |
| Inspiring From Within What? | 189 |
| Mindset Vacation | 192 |
| No Validation Required | 195 |
| Now What? | 198 |
| Wherever You Go, There You Are | 201 |
| Your Truth | 205 |
| Moments Of Truth | 208 |
| You Are Your Own Hero | 211 |
| Wrestling With Yourself | 214 |
| Mindset On A T-Shirt | 217 |
| What Can You Expect? | 220 |
| Where Do We Go From Here? | 222 |
| Wake Up And Think! | 227 |
| Influence, This | 230 |

| | |
|---|---|
| You Are How You Act | 233 |
| Changing Perspective | 236 |
| Guilt Works, Only Temporarily | 238 |
| What's Really Going On? | 241 |
| I'll Do It Later | 244 |
| As You Start To Walk On The Way | 247 |
| You Are One Decision Away | 250 |
| The Definition Of You | 255 |
| The Path Of Least Resistance | 258 |
| Trust Your Truth | 262 |

# Introduction

# Be Your Truth

Thanks so much for being here with me. The journey you're on isn't that dissimilar from my own. Most of us want the same things--love, happiness, security, experiences, and comfort in our own being--to trust and embrace who we really are. And, yet, who has all that, really? How do you tap into your soul to see what's there? Do you spend time thinking about who you really are?

Think about it. You weren't given a playbook or guide when you were born, and if you had been, there would be millions of iterations. The closest we have are faith-based books. And there are a lot of them. If that's not something you embrace, then you're back to zero. In any event, these books are someone else's opinions and perspective and not that of your own.

Sure, we get our information from a number of different sources. Some are helpful; some are not. However, what do you really know about yourself, your pure essence as a unique human being? Don't you need to first learn and discover who you are before embracing what others have to say?

We are constantly influenced by something or someone. The idea, however, is to gather as much information as you can and then form your own opinion. Do you do this? Or do you take most things as gospel? Yes, I'm asking you a lot of questions because I want you to start to think about what you really know about yourself.

What we tend to do is get so excited about other people's theories, ideas, ideals, doctrines that we start to worship and lean into everything that person has to say. This then no longer comes from our own thinking. We're now adopting another's point of view. This, over time, does not serve us well.

What happens when we do this is that we start to move into the shadows. We become less of who we are or what we need when we adopt verbatim others' opinions. Then we wonder why we're so confused or stuck or, worse, depressed. My intention in writing this book is to help you cut to the chase so that you can lead your best life and take decisive action. I'm here to show you that you may be getting it all wrong, to shed some reality on the decisions that you're making, and the people you think influence you. I'm here to show you "your truth."

More often than not, we are obsessed about the wrong things. We place far too much importance on what others have to say. Does this make any sense to you? In reality, we rely the least on ourselves. I've seen people *fake it 'til they make it* their entire lives. It's just getting worse. That can't be good. To set the tone for what you're about to experience, I'm going to offer you a different perspective, a different mindset, if you will, on how to lead a life where you're tapping into your truth of who you are and, also, recognizing through observation why you may not be getting any further ahead. I encourage you to have a notebook by your side when reading this book. There are lots of exercises that I hope will help guide you to your truth.

It is also my hope that you will start to recognize that by being on autopilot is just another way of saying that you have no idea what or where you should be-- or where you want to be going. I'm not talking about Instagram, Snapchat, Facebook, or any other social media platforms that you use or will use (that haven't been invented yet) that puts your best "fake self" forward. Nope. I'm talking about how to get to the place where you're saying: *Wow, my life is good without having to post ONLY the happy moments in my life.* And these, by the way, sometimes feel as if they're few and far between.

While we're on the subject, I equate social media to the picture frame that you buy in a store. You know the ones--with the model family or guy or girl that already comes with the frame. It's not real. At best, it's murky. It can give you a false sense of things. Also, it can reinforce just how depressed, anxious, and unhappy you actually are (or might be).

This book is broken down into various streams of thought and circumstances that I hope will spark a shift in you. I'm taking a Seinfeld-esque approach, if you will, where this has you reflecting upon your life through observation and experiences, taking you on a journey to finding your own truth. I hope this helps you to have a more meaningful and expansive look at the ways in which you can get closer to your real self.

When something really resonates with you and you think: *Yes! That's exactly how I feel* and yet you're not sure what to do with those feelings or what actions to take, that's where I will step in to help distill the noise, to help you get better aligned and more aware of your true actions and responses. You'll be far less conflicted and so much happier and certainly more grateful once you identify what's holding you back. You will discover that your truth is waiting to appear, that once you put your fears aside, you will begin to tap into your intuition. In doing so, you will finally get to a place where living on autopilot is no longer an option. You will choose YOU. In this choice you will start to take action toward leading the life that you were meant to be leading. That's what I want for you, and that's what I trust you want for yourself.

It's time. This is your **Call To Action** to be your true self.

# PART 1
# How Did We Get Here?

I've often wondered if we've given much thought to this question. Who are we really? From the moment we're born we're not 'us.' Not really. We're told who we are. It's not until we're able to stand on our own two feet that we discover more about ourselves. And, when, or if we do, is it really us?

# It Starts With You

## *Who is YOU?*

As you start to learn more about yourself and discover what gives you energy, what does it mean to be YOU?

How are you taking action toward "being" your potential? When do you start to trust yourself more? When do you start to recognize that it's within you to BECOME, to become your voice, to follow your flow and energy around your purpose?

You know **it starts with you--** when you're comfortable being your authentic self, your strong self, your vulnerable self, your confident self, your loving self. You know it when you can breathe within yourself. You know it when other people's opinions are just that-- opinions.

Once you gather your strength of being, that's when the magic happens.

Today is that day. What does that look like for you? It's important to note that how you show up in this world is how you will BE with others. Here's where I'm going with this.

I suggest you pause for just a moment and think about how you would describe yourself. Write it down. Now think about how you show up day to day. Are you aligned? If you were to be completely honest with yourself, do you walk the talk? We tend to be more attracted to the idea or function of something rather than have to action it.

For example, I was at a meet-up event where the topic was: *Being Present, Engaging and Connecting Authentically.* Interestingly, both the organizer and a few people on the panel were anything but present or engaging in conversation. UNTIL they were "on." They were unaware of their own self-awareness. I notice this happens a lot.

If you are to become a better human being, you need to start with yourself. You need to stop looking for answers outside of yourself. It's not about status and position. It's about leaving your ego at the door and entering a room with your heart, your soul, your true vibe. That's what others feel before you ever say one word. Bring it back to yourself. It has to start with:

Loving Yourself First. When you do, you are a much more loving person to others.

Being YOU. Let yourself show through. Show the world your unique talents. By being you, you will attract the right people into your life.

Listening. It is more important than talking. You need to learn how to hear what people are saying so that they can be heard.

I'm not saying it's easy. It's not. If it were, we would all be living wonderfully supportive and loving lives. I do, however, hope that one day your one mission in life would be to: *Wake up to connect and inspire with others so that others can rise.*

I have a dream ….

## To Be Your Truth:

Taking action toward understanding your truth.

Write this down:

What does the word "truth" mean to me?

How do I live this definition of truth in my life?

# Life As We Know It

I'd like to offer you a different perspective--mindset, if you will--on how to lead a life that works for you ... for REAL, where, after a while, you'll recognize that being on autopilot was just another way of saying that you had no idea how to get started. I'd like to offer you a way to take decisive action. We're so busy projecting and looking around and underneath ourselves that no wonder we're walking around shaking our heads saying, *Is it just me?*

Ok, yes, I do tend to be that person who sees the glass half full. That's only because I made my mind up when I was very young that the only person that was going to make me happy was ... ME. I imagine this came about or was due to the fact that I was quite disappointed with how words rarely translated into action.

I found that in order to make things happen in life, I had to take matters into my own hands--which I did. In hindsight, I was pretty pleased with myself. I remember when I was in high school, there were a number of us making plans to go skiing for March break. We needed to complete the forms and hand in our deposit to the customer service person at the lodge where we were planning to stay. As the weeks went by, I noticed that no one had sent in their form or deposit. When I asked about this, they said that they had decided that they didn't want to go. Some didn't have the money; others had an opportunity to go away with their parents.

Being ticked off and incredibly disappointed, I spoke with my parents. After all, I was only 15 and needed to ask them if I could go on the trip by myself. Initially, they were against it. After much conversation (more like my begging them), my parents said I could go with a few provisions. They knew I was a very responsible kid. I had demonstrated it time and time again.

They also knew how much I LOVED to ski. And, yes, they were certainly disappointed for me because my friends had bailed at the last minute. Was I happy about going on a ski trip by myself? Absolutely not. And yet I was determined to prove to myself that no one was going to hold me back from doing something just because he or she didn't want to do something with me.

The first day I arrived I felt incredibly lonely – painfully lonely – PAIN-FULLY. It was a horrible feeling. The first day I skied by myself. I could have easily called my parents to come pick me up, and they would have gladly come and gotten me. That would have been too easy. I knew I had to ride through this wave of loneliness. And then ... it happened. I saw a few people that I recognized from school, people that I hadn't hung out with before. They were happy to see me. They also couldn't believe that I had come alone. In their eyes I became super cool-- brave even! That week we had a blast. It was one of the best trips I have ever been on.

Actually, in hindsight, and I hadn't until this second recognized it. THAT, in fact, was a turning point for me. It was then that I knew that I was solely responsible for my own life, my own happiness. This created the confidence and courage for me to make other big decisions in my life going forward.

I declared to my parents one evening that I was going to travel around the world. Later, in my twenties, I did just that. I was gone for almost three years.

**So, what exactly is this shift in mindset? What perspective would I like you to consider?** In fact, it's quite simple. And, it's also quite terrifying for most. It comes down to YOU. You are the only one who can hold yourself back, back from the *What if's* in your life. Sure, you make excuses to yourself ... I'm going to guess...probably all the time. But, what if today, this moment, you chose not to hold yourself back? What if you chose to walk past fear and uncertainty to get to where you want to go--even IF you're not quite sure exactly what that looks like? What if in doing this it would bring you closer to discovering what excites you? After all, this is YOUR life--- no one else's. Even if you have children-- trust me--children need to see that you're taking responsibility for your own happiness. The other wonderful people in your life are, in fact, a reflection of how you treat yourself. **Don't settle.**

## To Be Your Truth:

Write down:

What's Holding You Back? Name one action that is holding you back.

Then take one action toward that one thing. Repeat often.

## What's In A Name?

Think about this. The moment we're born someone names us--our parents, a nurse, a guardian. Someone gives us a name. And it's not, *Hey, you*...well, not officially. Each and every one of us is given a name. Even if it's Jane or John Doe, we have a name. Having said that, do you then start to identify with that particular name? Did I start to think, *what would an 'Amy' do?* Would she play with Barbie dolls, climb trees, wear her hair short or, maybe, long? In fact, the people who looked after us for the first years of our lives typically handed us certain toys, styled our hair in a certain way, dressed us in clothes that 'they' liked.

Case-in-point--I remember my mom loved to put a bobby pin in my hair. Ugh, I really didn't like that thing. It bugged me. But, nope, she liked that my hair wasn't in my face.

Gee, our parents or caregivers even tinkered with our personalities. They taught us how we should behave, what we should say, how we should say it, and how we should act. So, really, *we're not 'us' just yet. Are we 'acting?* Is that it?

So, when exactly do WE show up in our own lives? Is THIS why we become so rebellious in our teens? Even then we're being influenced by our peers and people in the media. Have you ever really gotten to know yourself? Each and every one of us has been influenced by others. Come on. You can even make a living being an "influencer." Is our life the result of one big marketing spin? People make it their life's work trying to get us to *buy this, do that, go here, experience that.* If we don't, we feel as if we're missing out on something, which then makes us feel isolated and lonely.

I believe that we hit various 'panic' stages in our lives, when we're really rattled. We start to lose sight of who we really are, and this freaks us out. You may know what I'm talking about when I say, "the terrible teens," "midlife crisis," or name any other stage of life when we're thinking, *What am I doing with my life? Who am I?*

This identity crisis starts when we're born. If we don't give it the attention that it deserves, then we're doomed to lead a life that is dictated by others. **So, what are we going to do about this?** *I'll tell you what we're going to do about this ...* You see what I mean? Someone else 'telling' you what to do. Ok, all joking aside ...This is why it's so important to understand yourself better, to get to know who you are and what matters to you.

I'd like to suggest that you read and gather as much information as you can. Get informed and THEN make your own decision based on what's best for you. As you start to gather more information, you'll also notice a lot of contradictions--a lot.

Everyone has his own opinion. Who's right? Who's wrong? It doesn't really matter. What matters is that you're getting better informed, and when you do, you can then understand better what makes the most sense to you. I ask you, *What's in a Name?* YOU decide. No matter where you are in your life today, what your life conditions are, what your circumstances, ask yourself, *What do I want?* Take out any words or thoughts that start with *If only*.

## To Be Your Truth:

Think back to when you were young. Go as far back as you can remember. Start to think about how you were in your "most real" state. You being you. You playing. Interacting with your friends. What did you like to do? Where did you like to go? Write down what you can remember.

Amy Goldberg

# 5 Ways To Turn Your FOMO To JOMO
## *And then this happens*

And here lies the problem with not knowing who you really are:

Nope, FOMO and JOMO is not a new language. It's a mindset. Here is something to consider as you start to unravel who you are and what motivates you. A lot of it has to do with mindset. I've been reading a lot about FOMO (fear of missing out) and how thought leaders are asking us to consider the JOMO (joy of missing out). Inevitably, this shift in mindset should decrease our anxiety and create space for us not to feel overwhelmed and out of control. Can a change of mindset do all that?

Did you know that the average teenager spends around 6 hours a day and the average adult 4 hours a day refreshing his or her social media feeds? That's 37% of teens' and 25% of adults' waking hours being spent on social media. This obsession has led to a slew of health issues. FOMO comes from unhappiness. Getting caught in the FOMO cycle shows low levels of satisfaction. Hence, you ramp up your social media usage to make yourself feel better, and, yet, research shows that it actually makes you feel worse. To make things even worse, it's an addiction that's hard to break, and the tech companies know this. This is similar to the thinking of cigarette manufacturers.

Consider this: by turning your FOMO into JOMO, you disconnect; you opt out and you're actually OK just "being." It's about being present. It's trying to find some kind of balance and setting boundaries. So now what? What can you do to turn your FOMO to JOMO?

Here are a few things to consider:

**Acknowledge: "Do I have a problem?"** Yep, I can see a 12-step program in the future (if it hasn't been created already) on technology addiction. The first step is to take responsibility for your actions. So how do you know that you have an addiction? Let's see: (1) You feel the need to use your smartphone more and more often – you've tried to decrease your use and yet your attempts have failed. (2) You have a preoccupation with your smartphone, constantly on social media apps. (3) Your use is excessive, and you feel a lack of time for other things. You feel you are losing control of your life.

If you find that your smartphone is ruling you, try and keep track of your digital habits. There are apps that can help you do this. Some apps include: Social Fever, My Addictiometer, Quality Time, Space, AppUsage, App Detox, and OffTime

**Say "No."** Some of us have a hard time saying "no." Exercise your right to say "no." Think of it this way: the more you say no to things that you really don't want to engage in, the MORE you can say "YES"

to what really jives you. Also, begin to cultivate the expectation that you may not respond immediately to text and email messages. You don't have to be Quick Draw McGraw. Healthy boundaries are a good thing.

**Om.** Be in the moment. There's nothing more satisfying then being mindful of what you're doing in the present. You may have heard this before, and yet it's worth repeating: "The past is gone, the future is unknown, but what we do have is the present – and the present is a gift."

**Ignore Everybody.** Embrace JOMO. Don't believe that when you're not anxious or bored, you're guilty. By nurturing your creativity, you'll start to move into a state of following your bliss. This occurs when you're in the right state of mind. When you're away from devices, you'll find yourself thinking and doing more.

In shifting your mindset from FOMO to JOMO you will, over time, start to feel a sense of ease. You'll be able to breathe more freely again. It's not a coincidence that digital detox holidays and no social media wellness retreats are on the rise. There's a reason for that. People are finding that it's just too tough to go it alone. And yet, I promise you, if you take back control of your life and shift your mindset to the JOMO, you'll find your joy.

## To Be Your Truth:

Identify your fears. Just list them. Don't think that much about it. That's it. Once you've done that, leave it aside. Save it, however, as we'll be revisiting it.

Amy Goldberg

# What's Grounding You?

*It's ground-breaking*

As we talk about you and working toward discovering more of who you are, consider this. You are constantly thinking, planning, and obsessing. You may have heard through various internet sources that we make 35,000 decisions a day. I don't know if that's true, however, according to researchers at Cornell University (Wansink and Sobal) we make 226.7 decisions each day on just food alone.

Needless to say, you spend a lot of time in your head and tend to forget what grounds you. No wonder the root chakra when blocked can leave you feeling sluggish and stuck. However, when you gain connection to your root chakra; the first chakra; your grounding chakra, you better connect more soulfully with the earth and with yourself. This helps to clear your mind for creating space for what inspires you.

Have you ever heard the expressions *Be on firm ground,* or *Getting on your feet again,* or *To lose ground,* even *Getting swept off your feet?* These all convey a closed (or almost closed) root chakra. When your root chakra is closed too far, you may actually feel that your feet don't seem to be touching the ground. Moreover, when the ground disappears, and your feet are no longer planted firmly on the ground, it can leave your feeling anxious. This is directly tied to your physical vitality, endurance and mental perseverance. You essentially lose your security.

If the first chakra is unbalanced, inevitably, the rest of your chakras become unbalanced. Your first chakra lays the fundamental foundation for your entire system. Let me ask you this. Do you have a hard time putting your thoughts into action? Are you easily stressed? Are you restless? Are you fearful or constantly worried? These are all signs that your grounding chakra could be out of balance. What can you do to unblock your chakra?

Let's try this:

## **An Exercise:**

Here are exercises worth trying:

### **Grounding Exercise**

Your root chakra connects your body to the earth's energy. When your energy is blocked, you are unable to access the support of the earth and the higher awareness of your spirit. A simple grounding exercise helps to anchor you through visualization. Close your eyes. Now imagine that you are a tree. Visualize roots growing out from your feet and extending into the ground. Feel the sensation of being firmly anchored into the earth.

## Meditation

The one barrier to one not meditating has come down to time. People think that they need to dedicate a lot of time to meditation. In actual fact, you can meditate anywhere at any time for a few minutes. Meditation that involves bringing attention to your physical body will help to balance your root chakra. Do a body check-in by scanning each body part from head to toe (or toe to head). Become aware of your physical being. Take deep breaths bringing your awareness to what you are doing. When you are grounded, you are conscious of yourself, your surroundings and the earth.

## Physical Activity

Your root chakra is tied to your physical energy and vitality. Physical activity helps to remove any accumulation of toxic energy. Shifting your energy from your mental focus to your physical one clears the pathway in your mind and opens up your body's energy. You will experience a sense of well-being when you connect to your physical self. You will achieve this by doing any activity that increases your heart rate.

## Eat Grounding Foods

According to Ayurvedic Medicine, there are grounding foods that you can eat. These include potatoes, sweet potatoes, beets, carrots, green beans, eggplant, and ginger. Other grounding foods include avocado, mango, papaya, grapes, olives, berries, coconuts, figs, and melons. In addition, drinks should also be warm and not cold.

**Connect with Nature**

Allow your mind to take a break. Let it wander as you are out in nature or on a beach. If you are able to walk barefoot and feel the sensation of the ground beneath your feet, daydream. Did you know that some of our best ideas come from daydreaming? Enhance your experience by breathing deeply into your diaphragm. Try and stay in the moment.

As your root chakra provides grounding and support, it will help you to build the foundation for living an inspired and energetic life. Concentrate your energies on the present and direct your attention to your root chakra.

## To Be Your Truth:

Try doing these 5 exercises to help unblock your chakra. Watch as you will begin to feel more grounded, secure, and at ease with yourself. You will experience a positive shift in your energy.

# Change Happens. How Do You Handle It?

*And then this happens*

You know intellectually that change is constant, and, yet, emotionally and physically you don't always handle it so well. So, what gives? There is a perceived risk of fear associated with change, fear of the unknown. Just as you start to get comfortable with something ... change happens. When it does, your brain triggers fear or excitement. So, if that's the case why not trick your brain into thinking that you're excited rather than fearful or anxious.

Did you know that your body has the same physiological response whether you're fearful, anxious, or excited? The chemical release in your body is the same. Knowing this is the way you can begin to change your emotional experience of the situation.

**Here's an exercise** that you can do immediately to help: The next time you have a fearful reaction to a situation or a change in your life, raise your arms over your head (like a victory pose) and say**, "I AM EXCITED!"** Repeat this like a mantra. What's happening is that you're getting yourself out of a threat mindset in which you're thinking about all the things that could go wrong and into an opportunity mindset in which you're thinking about all the positive things that can happen. This little trick will help. Try it.

In order, however, to get better with change you need to learn to shift your behavior. In the long run, it's best to acknowledge and confront why you're uncomfortable. If you are becoming fearful or anxious, try changing the story that you're telling yourself. Ask yourself: *Why am I fearful? What's holding me back?* Then choose to focus on all the opportunities and positive outcomes that will come with this change. Over time you'll get better at it. It'll become your new learned behavior. Once you realize that change happens-- whether you're ready for it or not-- you will begin to build up your resiliency for change. Think of it this way – the more you experience in life, the more you have to offer. Now THAT'S exciting!

## To Be Your Truth:

Remember when you made a list identifying your fear? Now go back to that list and write beside each fear what's holding you back. What can you do to get past the fear?

Amy Goldberg

# I Now Know The Secret Of Success

## *Do we really know?*

Oh, no, not another *Secret of Success* thing! Had to. Felt compelled. This comes down to how you feel about yourself--the distractions that take you away from who you are and what you need to be doing for yourself.

Recently, I've been reading a lot about *The Secrets of Success from Billionaires, The Top 4 Things Billionaires Do To Be Successful, Fail Often: Memoirs Of A Billionaire. Billionaires: Let's Get Raw.* The common theme being: *Billionaires.* Apart from the fact that they're all billionaires, what else are you enamored by-- if, in fact, you are attracted to it? Do you care if they're kind, generous, helpful, philanthropic? I'm not sure. My sense is that you may be attracted to how they made their money-- hence, the reason why you gravitate toward and cling to the language of: *Get Rich Quick. Follow Me and I'll Show You How I Became Super Rich,* etc.

So, what is it that sets you apart from the elusive billionaire's club? Well, to purely cut to the chase, it's a number of things: it's your life conditions, circumstances, mindset, creativity, curiosity, tenacity, element of luck (yes, luck), whom you hang out with, and your disposition.

Maybe, even, if this is you, the preoccupation with how billionaires become billionaires is what sets you apart. It could be the *Why them and not me?* thing. Maybe it's because you give up way too early on yourself? Maybe you become impatient because you're not amassing wealth fast enough? That's probably why lotteries are so popular. And, yet, research shows that people don't fare well after winning a large sum of money in the lottery. So, what is it that you're missing? I think I now know the secret of success and it's …. *YOU*

*What? That's it? Just that?* **Yes.** It always comes back to **you**. You're the only one that can make anything happen for yourself. If I gave you a complicated answer, then it would just fuel the fire of stagnation. It would do nothing to ignite a fire under you just to take *action.*

I also know how to strengthen your odds of becoming (more) successful. What it's NOT is giving into limiting beliefs, a fixed mindset, negative self-talk, and relationships that don't serve you. Look, we all come from the same place. **It starts in our mind--** what you believe to be true for yourself. This is true whether you came from humble beginnings, sadly abusive or tragic conditions, or a privileged upbringing and circumstances. We all have the ability to succeed. Some have a much easier go of it than others. And yet we all have the opportunity to succeed.

Here's the thing: **Stop** looking around at what is perceived to be real. The half-told social media stories, images, lives that OTHERS are leading. **Start** diving into your own life. The excuses should end here-- today--right now. This isn't a pep talk. It's a reality check letting you know that you have the capacity for so much more, more than you realize. Just don't lose sight of the fact that you are on your own journey that spells S.U.C.C.E.S.S in your own life. Don't worry about the billionaires of the world. They have their own problems. Ok, so one of them isn't money. Start following your energy around what motivates and inspires you. Be relentless. Be kind. Be empathetic. Be bold. And, most important, start trusting yourself. Have the courage and confidence to push away the fear and move past it. You've got this.

On a side note, as a pure observation, have you ever noticed that people rarely, if ever, share their hard times while their IN it. They have no problem sharing EVERYTHING once they've made it. They'll share with you their most humiliating experiences and life events as they once struggled. Look, I get it. This is their way of connecting with the rest of us. What they're saying is: *If I can do it, you can too.* Sure, it's kind of a spin, and, yet, you shouldn't care. You have more important things to do. You need to **Be Bold. Be You.**

## To Be Your Truth:

Start listening and following your energy around what motivates and inspires you. Be relentless. Be kind. Be empathetic. And, most important, start trusting yourself. This is where you start to unravel your fears and start to move past them. This is not easy.

## Listen Up! It's Important

### *Where are you?*

What? What am I talking about? Every time we listen to ourselves, we get all messed up. We start in on ourselves with negative feedback, lazy internal conversations, self-destructive behavior, and a mindset that doesn't serve us well. My question for you is where are you in your life today? Are you pleased with who you are and what you're doing? Today. Right here. Right now. What's holding you back? Do the conditions of your life match the expectations that you have for yourself? What kind of expectations do you have for yourself?

So many questions-- and, yet, do you have the answers to them? It has to start with you.

As we move into a new year, now is a great time to reflect on and, yes, question where we are.

Consider this. Start leading your life by how you feel about what you're doing. Start listening to what your energy is telling you.

As you get deeper into this book, you'll see the title *You Know What You'd Be Great At?* I mention starting an energy log. I'm a BIG fan of this as it really does move you toward an action mindset. Start keeping track of what energizes you, what excites you. Also, write down when you're not feeling it,' when your energy is low or depleted. I bet after you do this for a month, you'll start to see patterns. It's a real tell. It'll start to reveal what your energy gravitates toward.

If you're finding that I repeat myself, I am. It's a deliberate action to ensure that this is ringing true for you. Driving the message home takes repeating. Having said that, you may be asking; *Why doesn't she let up on this? Why is she always harping on how I can be better, happier and thriving?* Apart from the fact that I care, the reality is that life throws you a lot. You need to gather information, new knowledge, and the tools needed to handle best whatever you're facing.

Guidance to help you along the way does prove helpful. You take what you need and discard what you don't. That's why it's always helpful to gather information from many different sources.

Sure, some of us are further along than others. I can't say that anyone has it all figured out. Nope. We're all humans with vulnerabilities. You need to start getting comfortable being vulnerable. This is when you'll start to see enormous growth in yourself. Your vulnerabilities tell you a lot about yourself. In turn, it will help set you on a better path.

The way to a happier life is first to see where you are right now. Does your life condition match the expectations that you have for yourself? If yes, great, keep going! If not, start to look at the changes that you can make given what you're able to do right now. Every day you act on the changes that you want to make will bring you closer to what you want. Head toward the direction that your energy moves you toward.

*Listen Up! It's important. You're too important not to listen to what you're trying to tell yourself. Start listening. Then act. Then keep going.*

## To Be Your Truth:

Start listening to yourself. Really listen. If you're not happy or satisfied in your relationships, work, home life, lifestyle, health habits, sleep patterns, (keep adding to this list) then you are NOT listening to yourself. Start NOW.

Amy Goldberg

# Love Made Us Do It

*Is love enough?*

During any holiday season our hearts are more open. We tend to share more, care more, and give more. It's a time of year when love is all around.

Love can make us do a lot of things. IS IT, however, powerful enough truly and unapologetically to love yourself wholeheartedly with compassion and admiration in the same way that you love others? Why is it that we are kinder to others than we are to ourselves?

What if you take that same love, that external love and send it back to yourself?

What if when you hear **Love Made Us Do It,** you 'feel' it rather than 'think' about it, truly 'feel' what that means to you? Right now, these could seem just like words, not really hitting a chord – or maybe it's hitting a chord, but you just don't know how to play it. You're not sure of the vibe just YET.

I know you know how to play it. If you're reading this, then I'm guessing you're interested or intrigued. Whatever the motivation is, it doesn't matter. We all show up in this life coming from different places in our lives, different mindsets, experiences, and emotions. Our journey is unique to us, and, yet, we are all on a journey. It's never a direct path.

And if it were, it would be boring. You would never know and learn how resilient you really are.

So, what do I mean by "Love Made Us Do It?" When you give yourself the same compassion, love, and care that you give to others, watch how you feel. In doing so, you're not only sending out more positive vibes that WILL make you feel more energetic and lighter. In turn, others will feel your vibe before you even utter a word. The reason that's so important is that we tend to flip this on its head. We expect the opposite.

Most of us expect to get our energy from others before we look to ourselves. We read people; we read rooms; we read vibes - first. I'll give you an example. I used to have on my calendar a daily reminder note that said: *Ask yourself in any situation, "Do I feel Energized or Depleted?"* I have since deleted that note because I recognized that IT'S UP TO ME to feel energized or depleted.

What if you started with yourself FIRST? When you perceive yourself in a kind, caring, confident, and loving way, watch how the world shifts for you. Take situations in your life in which you're feeling really good. You tend not to second guess yourself; you tend not to worry about what other people are thinking or saying. Now, take that same scenario in which you're not feeling good about yourself. Your confidence is low; you don't feel put together; you're feeling insecure and uncertain; you're just not feeling it. You now perceive things much differently. You may be looking over at someone who's looking at you and thinking, *"What are you looking at?"* And, hey, maybe that person was just about to compliment you on your great hair!

The energy that you get from yourself positions the way you feel about almost everything. How you feel will depend upon how you treat yourself and others. You may not necessarily be feeling the love all the time. You actually won't. And, yet, what you can do is work toward shifting your mindset – your self-talk. Your self-talk creates your reality. So, now, flip the switch – and start by building your confidence. Yes, you need to build your OWN confidence.

Here are 8 affirmations. Repeat these slowly. Ideally, every time you read one affirmation, raise your arms in the air like a victory pose. This exercise, repeated daily, will help to shift your mindset.

- I am capable.

- I know who I am, and I am enough.

- I choose to think thoughts that serve me well.

- I choose to reach for a better feeling.

- I share my happiness with those around me.

- I feel energetic and alive.

- I am confident.

- Each step is taking me to where I want to be.

How do you feel? Lighter? Energized? More confident? Nothing at all?

Don't give up. You're worth it.

Any holiday season is a time for reflection. It can also be a very stressful time. It's this stress that has you spinning. This is why you need to look to yourself. Rather than feel as though you are depleting your energy, PAUSE. Take a deep breath. You can and need to understand your mind better. You need to ask yourself, *How do I really WANT to feel?*

The only way is to start is by taking action, by not being afraid to discover who you really are, by being comfortable in being your authentic (real) self, your strong self, your confident self, your loving self. It's not easy if you haven't taken the time to get to know yourself. You may not "be there" yet. By that I mean you have not pulled back the curtain to reveal that, in fact, you are your own "Great and Wonderful best friend," and that is because life gets in the way. You're busy! *I don't have time to really get to know myself!* And, yet, you need to. You need to understand your mind better so that your actions reinforce how great you are. And you must not tug at your flaws. It's easier to criticize than to compliment.

When you have opportunities to gather together with others, you have the opportunity to connect and inspire with others so that others can rise. In turn, you rise. You shine. You feel a better connection to yourself and others. A sign that you're beginning to take action is when you know you can begin to breathe within yourself.

Trust yourself. Once you gather your strength of being, it is then that WE all start to become stronger, together. Today is that day because "LOVE MADE US DO IT"

## To Be Your Truth:

Find love in your heart. I don't care what it is or how small that spark is. Just find it and be it Every. Single. Day.

# Ready. Set. Go.

## *Are you ready?*

This might sound like a cliché, and, yet, this does resonate with me from a personal place. I hope it does for you, too. I've run 15 marathons so far in my life (a couple of Boston's). I say this as it never ceases to amaze me that running a marathon (any long-distance race for that matter) really does unravel some secrets to life. It's a metaphor for: *it's never over 'til it's over.*

In a marathon some tend to be impatient and start out much faster than they should in the long run. Some plod along, and, yet, if strategic enough and have trained for the distance, may catch the faster starter-outers. If you've put the proper training in, then it really is a mental game.

You need to pace yourself, not get psyched out by the faster runners (if you're smart you can even chase them down). You can't, however, be naïve in thinking that there isn't some maneuvering going on. You need to be prepared, nimble, flexible, and open to the reality that it does happen. People will try to trip you up. They'll attempt to push you out of the way so that they can get ahead. You need to be strategic and break the race down into a manageable pace so that the distance doesn't seem so daunting. You need to know that you have a reserve tank, and you need to learn how to use it.

On the flip side, this is a real opportunity to help others along the 'run.' When you see someone struggling, encourage him or her to keep moving. Let the runner know to keep putting one foot in front of the other. If one is new to the race, teach that runner to take 'water breaks' in order to stay hydrated. If someone reaches out to you before the race, guide that person to ensure that he or she has the proper gear for the race ahead. Suggest better ways to train so that the runner can avoid (decrease) injury.

I've translated this 'race mindset' into everything that I do or, at least, have tried to do in my life. I say this because I've seen time and time again people racing to get nowhere, fast. I encourage you to consider your life in a way that has you enjoying the distance (translation: the journey). Live at your pace and, yet, connect with a community that encourages you to keep going, to keep growing. Please remember that a 'runner's high' doesn't happen THAT often. When it does happen, enjoy it. Celebrate the moment. It's an incredible feeling. Similarly, life doesn't follow a straight line. Know that there are going to be challenges along the way. You're up for it because you're resilient; you've been training. You're learning and growing all the time.

I encourage you to pause to take in what you're doing. Encourage others to enjoy their journey as well. At the end of the race (our life)

Be Your Truth

we will look back and discover that **we have always been in this together.**

## To Be Your Truth:
It's never over until it's over. Together we're better. In your life, remember we are all energy. Play nice. Be kind.

Amy Goldberg

# Stop Kidding Yourself. Culture Matters.

## *And then there's the workplace*

*From the perspective of me (now) looking at this from a 50,000-foot entrepreneurial lens.*

Part of my journey is that I've been working for what seems to be a lifetime, trying to help companies create healthier, happier, more productive and inspiring workplaces--you know, a great working culture. My experience has proven that this occurs infrequently. Why? -- it's because it takes a real desire (and team) to <u>want</u> to create a great workplace. Because workplace well-being matters. *So, what does this have to do with "BE YOUR TRUTH?" It is time for all of us to create a happier, more enjoyable work culture.*

We actually owe it to ourselves.

You spend most of your waking hour going to some kind of workplace or multiple workplaces. Unhealthy workplaces can make you feel as if you're going mad. The workplace culture shapes your very being as you constantly need to navigate your emotions, your sense of who you are, and how you feel you "need" to act within your work environment. Quite frankly, it's exhausting.

If you're part of a more progressive generation in which you won't tolerate unhealthy environments, maybe you'll be the one to get it right? Maybe you'll climb up (maybe you're there already?) the corporate ladder fast enough to save us all. Unfortunately, it has to start from the top. It needs a champion, one that leads by example. It's sad and, yet, true. Hopefully, this mindset will shift when each and every one of us "brings it." Where we one day find that we love going to work.

I've always believed that together we're better. I wake up to connect and inspire 'with' others so that others can rise. It's not lip service. It's how I live my life. If I can't walk the walk, then I won't do it, say it, inspire it. Sure, I'm far from perfect. I wouldn't want to be, and, yet, too often I see leadership within organizations slinging in words with no meaning or action behind them. That's why I'm always surprised when someone actually delivers what they say they will.

If you truly want people to soar productively, personally, and professionally, then the lines shouldn't be blurred. They need to be blended in order to create a culture of care, trust, and inspiration. And then they need to mean it--*actually,* **Do it.**

A small example of this was when I was working with a few health start-ups who promoted themselves as 'experience leaders' within the health space--you know, the ones that call themselves 'disruptors.' And, yet, the culture was the complete opposite of that.

They hired and fired fast. Those left behind were completely unmotivated. Leadership actually said to their teams (I kid you not): *You don't seem stressed enough; I don't see the urgency in anyone working here; If you're going to work here, you have to live and breathe this; Of course, we encourage you to exercise ...* and, yet, they would look disgusted when people took breaks to do just that. It pained me to see this-- PAINED me.

As both an entrepreneur; encouraging well-being, and a business strategist, it was my role to point out and highlight these cultural inconsistencies to founders and CEOs. Once identified, I would then do something about it. When I did pinpoint the challenges, the founders were surprised by their behavior. They had little to no self-awareness. Zilch. The kicker was that they really didn't want me to do anything about it. It was a HUGE letdown for me. I really wanted to help make a difference. It was clear as day right there before my eyes, waiting for me to solve. Ugh!

I know I'm painting a bleak picture. Of course, they're not all bad. A lot are, however. Although I have been very fortunate to have worked with <u>amazing</u> people, businesses, and organizations from all sectors that did 'get it'(entertainment, government, education, community, corporate, private, not-for-profit, foundations, and start-ups), we still have a long way to go.

Forget the "for every dollar spent toward

employee health initiatives, $3-$5 are realized." It's a bogus number. The bottom-line is you NEED/MUST care about your employees. That means you need to decide how important your workplace culture is. What kind of culture do you currently have, and, more importantly, what do you want to create? How healthy, motivated, engaged, emotionally sound, productive, and innovative are you and your colleagues now? And, yes, there is always more that you can be doing.

From my experience I now know that no amount of work that I do will matter, nor is it worth it to work with organizations that have no intention of demonstrating their interest or are not ready to create a healthier, emotionally stable, and a happier work environment.

On the flip side, I do know that when organizations are serious about creating a positive culture, wow! magic happens, which equates to demonstrated results and new-found superpowers.

Please take heed of this – if you are planning to enhance, improve, completely turn your workplace on its head, you better have an actionable strategy or else it <u>will</u> backfire. You'll waste time and money, and your team will actually disengage, be unmotivated and emotionally spent if what you say is just the same old, same old. There's a reason why this saying rings true: **"Actions speak louder than words."** *My question for you is: "Where do you fit in? What kind of organizational culture do you want to create?"*

Amy Goldberg

## To Be Your Truth:

Stop kidding yourself. Cut the bullshit. Walk the walk. I repeat. Walk the walk or STOP talking.

# The Power of Listening
*I can hear you! Can you?*

When I was growing up, I thought everyone was an amazing listener. I thought that people were really intensely interested in what you said. You felt really heard.

Then I realized it was my mother and father who were amazing listeners. They were constantly praised for their incredible listening skills. People would go out of their way to comment on what great listeners they both were.

This is great, right! However, it was a crushing moment for me. I recognized how, in fact, most people were actually terrible listeners-- horrible. They were listening to answer and/or just wanting to talk. Many times, I felt hijacked in a conversation in which it was all one-sided, not only hijacked, exhausted.

The feeling of being really listened to is quite something. Have you ever spoken to someone who made you feel as though you were the only person in the world at that moment, who seemed truly engaged and interested in every word that came out of your mouth? How did that make you feel? Important? Understood? This is the power of deep listening. This is the power of being completely in tune with one's truth of who he or she is. Deep listening is more than a valuable social habit;

it is a transformative communication tool. With deep listening, you are not only allowing yourself the time and space to absorb fully what the other person is saying, you can actually encourage him or her to feel heard and to speak more openly and honestly. This is the key to developing rapport with others. Wow! I miss that.

Listening is the act of mindfully hearing and attempting to comprehend the meaning of words spoken by another person. I mean, do we do this? Listening is also a key ingredient for building strong leadership and healthy relationships. Listening takes a lot of practice. Even though we develop our ability to hear while still in utero, genuine listening is a skill that takes longer to develop. You can't really fake listening either. You need to be fully present. Listening takes eye contact, body engagement, and good questions. Genuine listening is to still your body and mind so that you can be fully present. No wonder people don't take the time to listen. It requires you to slow down.

Not everyone, however, deserves to be listened to. We tend to be turned off by those who are self-righteous, condescending, not willing to be open-minded, basing opinions on propaganda, performing rather than speaking from the heart. So, what is it to be a good listener? Here are some great quotes to motivate you to become a better listener... I hope this helps.

*I think part of my gift is that I love listening.* - Eric Clapton

Be Your Truth

*You never really understand a person until you consider things from his/her point of view.* - Harper Lee

*Wisdom is the reward you get for a lifetime of listening when you'd have preferred to talk.* - Doug Larson

*Listening is being able to be changed by the other person.* - Alan Alda

*Knowledge speaks, but wisdom listens.* - Jimi Hendrix

*When you talk, you are only repeating what you already know. But when you listen, you may learn something new.* - Dalai Lama

Do you feel heard? **I'm listening.**

## To Be Your Truth:

You already know what you know. By listening you just may learn something new. Go with that and start listening more.

Amy Goldberg

# You Know What You'd Be Great At?

## *Yes, you!*

For as long as I can remember, I've had the ability to listen, gather, and then relay to others *You know what you'd be great at?* with perfect accuracy. I could see the sparkle in their eyes when I said it out loud. My mentioning this is not to highlight my abilities. Not at all. It's to ask you, *why don't you know what you're great at?* If I know, then you certainly should, right? Well, not necessarily. I remember being so envious of those who knew exactly what they wanted to do in life. I thought, *Wow, they have it all figured out.* Me, I was floundering.

In actual fact, no one has it all figured out. Curve balls will still be thrown. Those that know, may know the direction they're coming from. But they're still flying. It's inevitable. For us, the only difference is that they're flying from all directions. In hindsight, always being 20/20, there were so many signs for me, so many clues as to, in my humble opinion, what I was great at. I knew one thing. I was great at telling other people what they were great at. Who knew that could be a thing!

Being mindful of what your instincts are telling you is an important factor in helping you discover what excites you, what inspires you, what ignites a spark in you. When speaking at colleges and universities, the #1 question I get all the time is: *I have no idea what I'm going to do after graduation.* I'm here to tell you that you don't need to know. You go to college and university to learn and grow. You're acquiring new skills. You're learning to think. You're gaining wisdom. You're maturing. You don't have to 'be' what you studied. Your major doesn't have to be 'that thing' you do for the rest of your life unless, of course, you know the profession that you're going into. One thing is for sure; pay attention to what excites you rather than chasing shiny objects. You will find your way when you feel your way.

### **An Exercise:**

One way to get started is to consider the following:

**Ask Yourself.** Look within. See what transpires when you look back and see what you instinctively enjoy doing. It comes easily to you. What comes easily is not always aligned with what you want to be doing, and, yet, it'll bring you closer to what you do want.

**Start An Energy Log.** Track when you feel energized and enthusiastic. Also, track when you feel drained. When you are engaged in activities that are in sync with your strengths, it's often invigorating. The opposite is true when you're not excited about something that you're doing.

**Take Action.** Get out and do things. Try things to determine better if it reinforces what you thought you'd be great at, or, perhaps, it's not sustainable enough to keep you energized.

**You As A Kid.** What did you gravitate towards when you were a kid? What did you like doing?

**Where Do You See Yourself?** Where do you see yourself in 5 years? I'm not talking about your career. I'm talking about what do you see yourself doing. This will trigger all the things you don't want to be doing. If you dig deep, however, it will reveal what you gravitate toward. Even if you're scared to death, don't let that stop you from really diving into where you see yourself. This is a big 'tell.' Please don't dismiss this.

**Write A Personal Manifesto.** This will help to align you better with what you want. It will help you to figure out what you care about, how you perceive yourself, and how you want to act moving forward. Use words like "I will," or "I am." Write it as you believe it to be.

If you're stuck let me know, and, yet, you've got this. Trust yourself. Don't let fear get in the way of what you want.

## To Be Your Truth:

Don't get ahead of yourself. Believe the dots will connect in your life. Have faith and trust your journey.

## Are You Ready For A Change?

*We're back to you again!*

Here's where you take all that you've read so far, the observations, the circumstances and situations in life, and start to shift your mindset in order to lead your life, your journey, your way, and take actions toward making it happen for yourself. Our mind is powerful. It's the center of our being. And, yet, it is not our being. Our brain moves us into action, and, yet, it can also hinder us. It can also paralyze us. We tend to believe everything that we think.

Think of your brain as a sponge, absorbing all that you gather, absorbing all that you've experienced and all that you've been shown in life thus far. We all have limiting beliefs, some more limiting than others, based upon life conditions and experiences unless, of course you have been given the magical powers of experiencing and understanding everything there is to know about life. Everything.

We all have biases. We all have egos. It's important to note that just because someone writes about something, speaks about it, and appears to be living a virtuous life, it doesn't make it true. Far too often we've seen quite the opposite. We've seen people in roles taking full advantage of their position misleading the public and, worse, doing harm and/or committing horrible atrocities. Where's our trust then? Gone.

Here lies the important element in order for each and every one of us to lead our lives in a way that resembles who we are and what we're capable of. You need to better understand who you are. You need to do a deep dive into how you got here this very day and where you want to be going. Despite the past and your journey, there are revealing elements that connect everything that you've done up until this point in your life. These stem from your life conditions, your upbringing, and the people in your life that have both negatively and positively affected your very being.

When you're young you don't know that you have the wherewithal to determine what's best for you. You have no idea what triggers you to respond with optimism or pessimism. When I was growing up, my twin brother and I were very different. We were yin and yang. I was a very positive and happy-go-lucky kid. I said *Yes!!* to everything. When my parents asked if we'd like to go here, there, wherever, I said *Yes!* That was my response even before they could finish their sentences.

My brother on the other hand was not on the same page. His go-to answer was *No.* He was happy just to be at home. When he wasn't at home, he was out playing tennis. I'd ask if I could come with him. Every time he said *No.* Every time. When we did go out as a family, he was a control freak. Yes, freak. One example of this was when we went out to get ice cream. My Dad's "mystery trips" always ended with us getting ice cream – yay!! However, my brother would stare at me while I ate my ice cream. It would drive him crazy every time I made a noise while licking my ice cream. He would become agitated and start yelling at me. I shook my head every time wondering what was up with him.

And yet, to this day, whenever my brother tries to control a situation or what I'm saying, it still triggers me. I'm reminded of our earlier days with the ice cream. We remember everything whether we realize it or not. It sucks. However, now I'm mindful of the trigger and let it go, knowing that it's "his" problem, not mine. Now that's knowing my truth.

## To Be Your Truth:

Don't be the answer for other people. Let them worry about themselves. Be your truth. Write down: *Where do you want to go? What do you want?* It may change. So what? At least you have a direction.

Amy Goldberg

## Excuse Me

Believe it or not, a part of becoming who you are and to "Be Your Truth" is how you show up in the world. When you start to become your truth, you actually are a nicer, more caring person. You're not a dick. You're not self-absorbed and leading your life with your ego or the sense of being entitled. In fact, these are all contradictions of who you naturally are. So, when I observe people not being aware of their environment, not being in tune with others, then I know they have not arrived at their truth. They can't be.

Here's an example of this:

Yes, I once found it annoying hearing, after maybe the 50$^{th}$ time, Steve Martin say in his 1977 stand-up comedy album *Let's Get Small*, "ExCUUUUUUse ME!" ….. Now, I miss it. I really miss it. Have you noticed that very few people say *"excuse me"* politely any more? It's as if those words have completely left the English language.

*Why is that? When and why did we abandon "excuse me?"*

Maybe it's because "excuse me" is also used on many occasions sarcastically and, hence, it doesn't sound as sincere when asking to move past someone? Maybe we're more afraid that someone will misinterpret our meaning as being rude rather than our trying to be polite? You know, I actually don't believe any of these excuses for a second. Ha, actually, not to use "excuse me" is an "excuse." I couldn't resist.

*I'm baffled.*

It has frequently been quoted that 93% of all daily communication is nonverbal. And yet, in fact, according to Dr. Albert Mehrabian, author of *Silent Messages*, he conducted several studies on nonverbal communication and found that 7% of any message is conveyed through words, 38% through certain vocal elements, and 56% through nonverbal elements (facial expressions, gestures, posture, etc.). Subtracting the 7% for actual vocal content leaves us with the 93% statistic. The fact of the matter is that the exact number is not important. The important part is that most communication is nonverbal. In fact, nonverbal behavior is the most crucial aspect of communication. And yet, stats or no stats, bumping into or reaching across or walking by ones eye line without saying a word is just plain rude in my opinion. And it drives me crazy. I am driven to the point of saying *"excuse me"* for the person, and now I'M not being pleasant. I'm now being rude. And yet, truthfully, that's how I feel. I don't want to have to interpret someone else's move when they could quite simply say *"excuse me."* I mean, hey, I don't know what you're doing. I don't know what you want-- not even to get a grunt! Am I supposed to be a mind reader?

Why do we seem to tiptoe around these words? If you don't like the words "excuse me," "pardon me," or any other polite words that gesture that you want something, then let's make up a new expression. You know, as Jerry Seinfeld did in one episode of "Seinfeld" in which he replaced *God Bless You* with *You are so good looking.* Would that work?

It's a simple resolution to a simple quandary. The fact that I need to mention this is bewildering to me, and, yet, I felt compelled. The idea that we need to write about, talk about, remind oneself, or even teach others to be nice and polite feels like a setback. How disappointing that we cannot muster enough breath and/or pause for a moment to be polite.

I'm asking you or, perhaps, you can ask yourself the next time you reach across or want to walk past someone to think, hmmmmm I should just say *"excuse me."* Now THAT would be the polite thing to do. That would be coming from a real, authentic YOU.

*Just sayin'*

## To Be Your Truth:

Your actions are a reflection of your truth. Every time you're not consistent with what you declared to be your truth, then there is a disconnect. This disconnect can cause unease. Practice being your truth by being thoughtful to others.

Amy Goldberg

## Asking The Hard Questions

I was recently asked about my own journey in life--questions like *What do I value?* As I started to answer what I valued, the first word that came out of my mouth was *truth.* From there I was asked *What does 'truth' mean to you?* We were drilling down to the essence of what I truly valued. As we were talking, or shall I say as I was talking, I saw that as I was hearing these words come out of my mouth, they had to be my deepest truth, or why else would I say them?

It was almost as if I started to feel detached from my words. I wanted to make sure that I wasn't just spewing out words that had no true meaning for me. I thought about it. After all, there are times when I speak my truth and don't always lead with my best self. I talk about truth, kindness, love, fairness, compassion, and equality. And, yet, I'm not always displaying these things. Perhaps the reason is because I sometimes get so angry, yes, angry, when I experience and/or witness people NOT being these things. I think why am I the one who is walking the walk when a lot of the time people are walking right into me? Literally. Why am I dodging, maneuvering, and throwing up my hands to other people's lack of care and interest in their fellow human beings? This is what I'm thinking.

There are days when I utter under my breath, *You're a fucking idiot.* That's my truth on THAT particular day. Yes, I think that!

Stepping back, I understand that I'm passionate about my values because it bothers me that others aren't as thoughtful. I really don't care that you're deep in thought or distracted. When you're out in the world, BE in the world. Present. Aware. Kind. Compassionate.

I kid myself when I say, *It's ok. It doesn't bother me. I'm bigger than my problems and all of that bullshit.* And, yet, in real life we are constantly interacting in one way or another unless, of course, you've barricaded yourself in your home never to be seen again. As I'm talking about my values, I'm noting that words are powerful. Powerful. They shape the expression of us. So, why then am I walking by stores that have messages of love, compassion, joy, inner peace, to find that the experiences IN the store are anything BUT the messages they conveyed?

The messages and behavior around the messages are opposite. So, when I go back to my first value being "truth," I want to make sure that I value it in a way that echoes my behavior. This applies to you and your life. If you are espousing the value in which you embody, then BE that. If you experience the opposite, then you need to re-evaluate and/or start to shift your mindset.

Imagine if everyone paused and considered what it meant to be a human being living in a society that we created. We are all responsible and accountable for our actions. Period. I can't imagine why anyone really wants to be an idiot. They're not really. They're simply struggling with themselves, with their anger. It's our life conditions and circumstances that have either derailed and/or convinced us that we need to be this way. That is why we are not practicing kindness, respect, or living our truth. The truth is that fear can take over our lives if we let it. When we are fearful, we are resistant to taking action. Any positive action that could better us is squashed by our own lack of respect and love that we have for ourselves.

I was speaking with a woman who mentioned that she was paralyzed to lead her life because she was brought up in such a negative environment in which she was told on a daily basis that she was no good. Imagine that! Imagine being told repeatedly that you're no good by a person that you expect to have your best interest at heart. Take a step back in time and you'll see that that person telling her that she was no good was, I'm sure, told the same thing by his/her parents. And so it goes-- until she breaks the pattern.

This starts with you. This is why boundaries are so important. Did you know that the happiest people are the ones that set the most boundaries? Why? -- because of the very reason you're told on a daily basis that you're no good. How could that possibly serve you well? How?

When I say that you need to ask the hard questions, I mean that you really need to ask yourself the hard questions. This goes back to the first question: *Who are you?*

As I'm writing, I'm looking around at the many people walking by, those on their phone, talking with others, distracted. The first thought is not *What are you thinking?* It is *What are you feeling?*

## To Be Your Truth:
Asking the hard questions will have you thinking about what you value. When you start with that, you'll start to understand what you need to do to shift your mindset to become consistent with who you are and what you stand for.

Amy Goldberg

# 5 Ways To Take Action

What's going on in your brain between the time you say yes to doing something until the time you perhaps have a change of mind. Well, let's see. For a split second, do you think you're going to do it, or do you already know that you have no intention of doing what you said you'd do? I'm fascinated every time I hear someone say *"yes"* to doing or showing up for something when in actual fact they have no real intention of taking action.

Is it fear of disappointing another, being stuck, uncertainty about what to do, laziness, or, maybe, it's a combination of all these? In any case, it's something certainly to think about and, hopefully, act upon... At the very least, it will help you to understand yourself better.

I equate *saying yes, when you really mean no* to someone who is always late for everything, you know, the ones that keep you waiting. Translation: it's a lack of respect for one's time. However, to give the benefit of the doubt, I don't believe most people intentionally want to waste your time. This relates back to the person and their struggle with their own time.

And, yet, I don't know about you, but when you say yes to something, I believe you. I'm excited. I'm thankful. I feel good. You have given me a gift of your time. Therefore, when you have no intention of doing what you said you'd do, you are now wasting my time. After all, I am waiting for you to do what you said you'd do. I'm even waiting for you to let me know if you can't do what you said you'd do. In the meantime, I'm not asking anyone else. I'm anticipating that I'm going to receive some kind of action from you.

***Do you see what I mean?***

Obviously, I'm bugged by this. I have conditioned myself to expect that something may not transpire if someone simply says that they'll do it-- sad but true I just may be losing faith in one's *good word, the handshake,* and *my word is my bond* statements. At the very least I have managed my expectations as I hate-- yes, hate-- being disappointed. It bums me out. I know I'm not the only one that feels this way. I know. I know. You may be thinking, *Suck it up; Life is full of disappointments.* And, yet, what a waste of time! And it is most likely an inconsistency in what you've declared to be your truth. I'm sure of it. So, what does any of this have to do with **5 ways to take action?** I'm a firm believer in **How you do one thing** *(most of the time)* **is how you do everything** *(most of the time).*

This means if you're saying *yes* to someone or something when you really mean *no,* or when you're known for always being late; or, for that matter; if you keep a messy home, car, or even computer, more often than not, other aspects of your life will probably be about commitment issues, procrastination, disorganization, or even having a scattered brain. I'd like you to consider where you are with this. Think about how you are in taking action toward leading a kind, proactive, and purpose-driven life. By working backgrounds, you can better determine why you may not be as action oriented as you may think you are or could be.

Consider the following ***ways to action*** and IF you're finding that you're stuck and not as motivated as you could be. Think back to how you do things most of the time.

*Here we go ....*

**Shorten The Thinking Process:** When you overthink something or get bogged down in the process, you can get overwhelmed. For example, when it comes to doing something that is 'good for you' you tend not to want to do it. You get lazy. In this case you need to 'leap' into action. This is a 'just do it' moment. The same thing goes for when you say *'yes'* to something while in the moment. In this case you can shorten the thinking process by better understanding your priorities. If you already know that you're overly committed, keep it short and simple, and just say *no*. You'll do everyone a favor in the long run.

**Don't Fixate On Outcomes**: When you put more of your brain power and focus on achieving your end goal, it can distract you from what you need to be doing in the moment. By fixating too much on an end goal, you might miss out on opportunities in the present. You need to be flexible to the possibilities as they arise.

**Eliminate Sources Of Distraction**: Distractions can take many forms--watching TV or a movie, taking phone calls, texting friends, even snacking. All of these can sabotage your efforts to get things done that you said you'd do. It's not about willpower. It's about removing the distractions that can lead to procrastination. Ideally you want to eliminate any temptation for distraction. For example, turn off your phone and the TV, and scale back your use of social media.

**Don't Wait For The Right Time**: There will always a reason not to do something. Always. There will never be the perfect conditions. Therefore, you need to do it anyway.

**Find Purpose**: All good actions have a reason and purpose behind them. When you find something that gives you purpose, finding that motivation to do it will be a lot easier. Purpose fuels the fire. Even when there are snags, if you go back to why you're doing something, it'll keep you going. It'll be easier to move through the tough times. Each and every one of us has goals and dreams that we want for ourselves. We may not know how to achieve them or how to get there, and, yet, I can say for certain that those things will be determined by the actions that you take in order to get what you want.

There's something to be said for the old adage *Better to take action and do the things that you want now rather than to wait and risk its never happening at all.* And there lies the truth. **What are you waiting for?**

## To Be Your Truth:

It's time to stop kidding yourself and start bridging the gap between what you say you'll do and what you actually do. It's time to take action--for real.

## What's It All About?

Interestingly, it all started for me when I became acutely aware that perhaps I was holding myself back. I recognized that I needed to step away from myself. Why was that, I wondered?

I knew, as human beings, we are our own worst critics. We tend to look around ourselves rather than tap into who we are. It's easier that way. We tend to play it "safe." As I considered how I was feeling, I knew that I needed to face my real self, the self that sometimes hid behind the self-assured, openly enthusiastic, action-driven person that I appeared to be. Why did I feel I needed to dive in and reassess where I was, what I was doing, and how was I feeling? What triggered my need for a revised look? Could it be that my self-diagnosed "deflectoritis" was getting the better of me?

Definition: DEFLECTORITIS
*The tendency of one who when asked a personal question, follows it up with another question so as to not have to answer the initial question.*

This tendency appeared not so long ago when I was at a crossroads in my life, not knowing exactly what my next move would be or where it would take me. My childhood, not unlike millions of others' childhoods, was a confusing time. I didn't know what I wanted to do or where my future was headed. When you're young, you think you need to have it all figured out. Happily, I now know that's not true. There were certainly things which I was determined to do. And, yes, I did them.

I started my first business while I was going to school; travelled around the world for just shy of 3 years and came back to start another business. I honed my skills as a writer, producer, artist, entrepreneur, and well-being professional – all the while seeing where the dots connected in my life. One thing was for sure, and I knew this at a very young age; I hungered for anything creative.

When I was a kid, people would ask me what I liked to do, and I said, *Anything creative!* They'd then ask, *What, exactly?* I didn't know. I only knew that I had to express myself creatively. And, then, of course, being an active kid, I needed to feed my passion for all things health & fitness related – and not only for myself. I needed to help others – bug, was more like it. I wanted to motivate people to move more, to rethink their behavior in a way that would prove more healthful to them.

Early on in my life, I navigated two worlds -- entertainment and health. I read scripts at night and delivered health prevention and lifestyle strategies by day. My brain was wired. I think the need for me to do so many things, where I felt pulled in so many directions, was my way of *trying* everything and anything to see what would stick. Upon reflection and deeper soul searching, I am, for the most part, able to get off the hamster wheel and better define what it is I need and want to be doing. The wisdom that I've gathered from others and the many experiences that I've had (and continue to have) have really allowed me to hone and, perhaps, reaffirm that *Hey, I'm on the right path.*

I was never really lost although *feeling* as if you're lost is just as tough as actually being lost. There are many moments in one's life where you need outside support from someone or something that can offer you the gift of validation and/or kind honesty. I find this most helpful when you know the path you want to take. This happens when you embrace the idea that *you're ready.* What I'm suggesting is that you trust and believe in yourself and your abilities. Stop and take a good look inside yourself for what is true for you. Try things. Experience as much as you can. And know that *You've Got This.*

## To Be Your Truth:

The only way to determine where you want to be going in your life that best defines your truth is to experience much and try things--a lot of things. Then you'll know what suits your soul.

Amy Goldberg

# Boss Is Not Boss

*Stop the madness*

What does this have anything to do with Be Your Truth? -- a lot. What we're told and what we say reflects how we are and shows up in this world as our truth. We need to learn to think for ourselves. We have a lot of the answers. We need to stop following other people, and what other people tell us to say.

I hear the word "boss" everywhere. Contrary to the urban dictionary definition of *That's Boss,* meaning awesome!! I'm here to say that the word "boss" is nothing BUT boss. For as long as I can remember, every time I heard someone utter the word "boss," I had a visceral response. It conjured up images of submissiveness, hierarchical behavior, upper hand, barking orders, ego, and one having no voice.

Interestingly, I have had no horrible experiences in my life in which the word boss would have solicited such a reaction. And, yet, I just knew in my entire being that the word should never be used ever again--not EVER. Is it my entrepreneurial free spirit that makes me believe in a collaborative approach where everyone has a voice and needs to be heard? Or is it my hang up with titles that makes me feel they tend to keep one in his or her place and stifles creativity? Partly, yes. And, yet, *Did you know* that the origin of the word "boss" originated from a Dutch word "baas" that means "master?" Ah, THAT'S why I truly despise that word.

According to Gifford Thomas, founder of Leadership First, *its use was a uniquely American way of avoiding the word "master," which had quickly become associated with slavery by the mid-19th century. Have you ever heard the phrase my boss is a slave driver? Note the words boss and slave. In those days many workers were fond of using boss primarily because they despised calling their superior master. But all their efforts were in vain because the connotation of the word remains the same despite all efforts to normalize its existence.*

It's unimaginable to me that people STILL, to this day, use the word boss interchangeably with leadership. The two are entirely different. Ironically, I read an article entitled, *The Best Bosses Have These Three Skills* with a tagline *The most effective bosses are the ones who give their employees permission to slip up.* Huh? Read that back to yourself.

Does anyone other than me see the irony of this? Doesn't this sound pathetically submissive and ridiculously condescending? Notice how they liberally interchangeably used boss and leadership. There is no LEADERSHIP in this article when the words "permission" and "boss" are used everywhere on the page. *Give Permission?* What are we-- 5? They've just set us back 100 years. *It's time to rethink what we're saying.*

**So, what can we do about it?** Let's start educating ourselves. Let's not use words just because everyone uses them, particularly when the context of the word is the complete opposite of what one is trying to convey.

By contrast, a leader is there to listen, to create a culture for everyone to collaborate and engage, a culture where people can thrive. Does the b-word say any of that? If we continue to use words like *boss,* think about how we're limiting ourselves and our beliefs. Let's not become complacent. Let's think and then take action. *It starts with each and every one of us.*


## To Be Your Truth:

Stop being complacent. I'm positive you know when something doesn't sit right with you. Just because you hear a word repeatedly doesn't make it right. Trust yourself. Know that it's not OK to just nod in agreement.

# Why?

I do a talk called: *Believe The Dots Will Connect.* It was 30 years in the making. Yep, true. It's about our journey in life, what it's all about, what we are supposed to be doing, and why we haven't figured it out? Rest assured; you're not alone in this. You hear a lot about finding your *why*. Personally, I feel the *why* is overrated. Don't get me wrong. It's important to know your *why*. However, I think we get too bogged down in trying to figure it out.

Rather, instead, I'm suggesting you try something a little different. If you start really to listen to yourself -- void of outside distractions, influences, and noise-- you'll start to take action toward *that thing* that thing that jives you. THEN you'll start to say, **Ohhhhh, that's WHY.** You see what I mean? There are clues everywhere in our lives. But where? How? Where do you start?

OK, so let's dig a little deeper into what that could look like for you. In working with people I've learned that we tend to put ourselves on autopilot. In fact, we've been on autopilot for so long that I bet many of us can't remember who 'we' really are.

The bigger question is *Have you ever really gotten to know the real you?* I'm guessing that we spend more time trying to find a show on Netflix then we do take the time to figure ourselves out. Sadly, it takes a catastrophic event before we decide to wake up to ourselves. It's not easy putting the pieces together. We have a lot of history being *us,* the *us* we think we kind of, sort of know. With all of this comes a lot of memories-- good, bad, and ugly that have been tattooed in our brain.

Look, you're not going to solve all the mysteries of *you* in one sitting. It takes time--years. Some may never do it. And, yet, I'm here to reassure you that you are not lost. You just need to look in places that you haven't gone before. It has to start with you. It has to start by writing down all the things that you're **NOT** willing to do. Yep, I said it--NOT willing to do. I find when you start weeding things out first, it gets you a lot closer to what it is that you want for yourself. Once you sit down and begin the process of taking action toward what it is that puts a smile on your face, then things will start to unravel positively. No one said it would be easy as you start listening for those vibes that give off a vibration that only you can hear. They're there. Start trusting yourself more.

The *you* that you should be focusing on will reveal itself once you're open to receiving. This isn't woo woo stuff. This is a process by which you need to take action in order to change the course of your life, in which you're thriving, not surviving. Start taking steps toward yourself.

## To Be Your Truth:

Start by writing down all the things that you're NOT willing to do. In doing this, it will get you a lot closer to what it is that you want for yourself. Trust yourself.

Amy Goldberg

## Are You Lonesome Tonight?

Did you know that loneliness is becoming a public health issue? Actually, being more connected has brought us further away from one another. We may be feeling disconnected and less motivated to build meaningful relationships as we start to isolate ourselves from the outside world. That's a problem. Social isolation is a growing health concern, both physically and emotionally. It can cause stress, increased blood pressure, diabetes, depression and speed up cognitive decline due to a lack of intellectual stimulation.

In May 2018, a survey conducted by Cigna, a large health insurance company, asked over 20,000 American adults if they agreed with statements like: *People are around me but not with me* and *No one really knows me well.* The survey, in particular, found that young people were lonelier than older adults. The study revealed that Gen Z (ages 18-22) and Millennials (ages 23-37) were lonelier and claimed to be in worse health than older generations.

The study went on to say that social media use alone was not a predictor of loneliness. In fact, ironically, many turned to social media as a way of treating their feelings of loneliness. Other lifestyle factors were also tied to loneliness, including disruptive sleep patterns, how much one worked, and how much time one spent with family.

Another lifestyle factor that had an impact on loneliness was physical activity. Those that got the right amount of exercise were considerably less likely to be lonely. And, yet, research showed that <u>too much</u> exercise could cause an increase in loneliness. It really comes down to a lack of balance--you know, too much of a good thing and all of that. Not surprisingly, those who engaged in frequent meaningful in-person interactions had much lower loneliness scores than those who rarely interacted with others face-to-face.

### *So, what's really going on?*

Researchers have defined loneliness as *perceived social isolation* with the key being *perceived*. Loneliness is subjective. It's the gap between the relationships that we have and the relationships that we want. Additionally, according to one theory, it all depends on what we believe to be "normal." If our social life looks like what we'd expect for someone of our age, then we're less likely to feel lonely. For example, *A teenage girl may feel lonely if she has only two good friends, whereas an 80-year-old woman may feel very connected because she still has two good friends,* says researchers Maike Luhmann and Louise C. Hawkley.

If loneliness is more about our state of mind, then we need to create more internally focused strategies. This, by the way, is where mindfulness and meditation can play a significant role in helping to quiet (so to speak) our feelings of loneliness. One thing is for sure, more research is needed to better understand both loneliness and isolation. And yet, both are equally bad for our health.

***What can you glean from this? It's important to nurture our connections with others.***

## To Be Your Truth:

When you start to take the time to find your truth, you will start to see what it is that you need from relationships, connection, and other areas of your life that will become your truth. It's when you're not sure, you feel lonelier. Get closer to your truth.

## You Have To Do It To Feel It

As I'm writing this, sweat is dripping from my body; my face is red; my heart is pumping fairly quickly, and I'm jacked. It was a choice not to wait to write this later after the feeling had diminished. I'm writing this now so that I'm better able to describe the feeling in real time.

As a runner, sometimes I forget why I run. It's not all about the physical activity. I get such a strong sense of empowerment and clarity when hitting the ground running (literally). Nothing else makes me feel the way running does. In the last 30 years, I've taught <u>every kind</u> of fitness class there is. Sure, I feel amazing after a workout. Of course, when I teach, I love that those taking my class feel fabulous, and, yet, I have never felt the same rush as I do when I'm running. Certainly, the endorphins kick-in with other activities, but it's not the same feeling.

*Here's the thing ...*

I don't always feel great when I'm running. It's tough. It's psychologically tough to get out the door, even when I KNOW I'm going to feel great once I step outside. However, when I do get out there, I feel, every-single-time whether it's a super tough run or I'm in the zone, a sense of freedom from my mind. Any sort of worry, concern, and/or challenges that I have going on seem to disappear when I'm running. In that very moment I feel so sure of myself that I invite "all" to *bring life on. Give me what you've got* because at that very moment I feel invincible. I feel that I can handle anything. It's a feeling of simplicity AND clarity at the same time. This isn't a runner's high. I've had runner's high before, and although that's a fantastic feeling, it's not the same. It's also not a "Rocky" moment where I'm going into the ring-- not at all. It's a feeling of *I'm great. Life is great. I don't need anything else.* And that is such a good feeling.

It's then that I am so very grateful that I have my health, that I'm strong, and that I'm able to run because THAT does it for me. What I also find incredibly interesting is how I feel when I don't run. My mindset is different. It feels different to me. I feel draggy, even foggy.

What works for me and helps to set the tone for the kind of day that I want is that I HAVE to exercise every morning. It's a priority. This is non-negotiable. The great thing about knowing oneself is knowing what works. It's so individual. It's true that when I don't run, the other forms of activity that I do leave me with a different kind of feeling, and, yet, it's still a great feeling. I'll take it! I look at it this way-- sometimes you can get too much of a good thing. Feeling the way I do when running (when I do run) is a great thing. It's a bonus.

I'd like to leave you with this thinking and invite you to check this out further if you're interested. I'm positive you already know about the benefits of physical activity, and, yet, interestingly, researchers at Oxford and Yale did a study of more than 1.2 million Americans. They discovered physical fitness is more important to your mental health than how much money you make. It plays into your emotional wellbeing. As my sweat starts to dry, my face is less red, and my breathing becomes relaxed, it's now time to hit the showers.

## To Be Your Truth:

Whatever feelings you have toward exercise, do it anyway. Start by moving more. You may not like it. But try it. If you've already embraced the exercise movement, great! Ask yourself: *How do I feel before, during and after exercise?* Where's my head? Finding your truth is as simple as asking yourself how you feel when in motion.

Amy Goldberg

# Love

What is it about love, particularly when we write about love, that turns us off? Is it too close? Too personal? Too mushy? Too feminine? Too much feeling of expression? I'm trying to figure it out. I'm not talking about sex. That's an easier sell. I'm talking about 'love.' On this subject, interestingly (more for me than you), I've been told that I am 'love.' Yep, I have. And what exactly does that mean? Again, it's not about sex. Sorry.

Ironically and admittedly, I was a late bloomer. I was naive in fact. I'm twin to a brother, a situation that had me feeling as if I were *one of the guys. Boy, was I wrong. That idea was only in my mind.* An example of this was one day (when we were in high school), my twin brother said to me: *Aim, my friend has this great tennis racquet that I REALLY want. The only way I'm going to get it is if you'll go out on a date with him.* I said, *What?* He repeated himself very matter-of-factly. When I didn't say "Yes," he begged me--for a week. You see, my brother was a seeded tennis player. He LOVED tennis, lived and breathed tennis. So, for him to trade me for a racquet seemed very reasonable. He truly thought 'I' was nuts for questioning him. But I digress. Even though you may want to know what happened, that's for another day.

All this is to say that I have always lived my life with love. I didn't know that's what it was. I just knew I had empathy; my heart was kind, and I struggled throughout my life whenever I experienced someone not being kind to another. I had zero tolerance for it. Why is it that we speak of love? We want love. Love is all around (and all of that), and yet we really aren't walking the walk. In my perfect world we would lead with our hearts. We would pause before we spoke. We would be thoughtful in the words that we chose. We would be the Shakespeare of the world, eloquent and kind, genuine and open-hearted. Why is that so farfetched? The truth is love truly does conquer all. Until we really understand it, we are fumbling around trying to figure it all out. If I can leave you with one thought, one consideration, try leading with your heart for one day. Maybe, just maybe, that one day will turn into many.

*Just think about it!*

## To Be Your Truth:

Pause. In order to be your truth, you need to pause before you speak. This will give you time to feel what's in your heart. Try leading with your heart. Trust me. It will feel quite different from when you were leading only with your thoughts.

Amy Goldberg

# Who Are You?

The band THE WHO have a great song called WHO ARE YOU, and it includes within the lyrics, *I really want to know*. I have many thoughts on this subject. I don't know about you, but, when I was young, the focus was never really about who I am as an individual but more around what I needed to do. It appeared to be so systematic, so regimented. I don't recall anyone sitting me down to talk about better understanding who I was as it relates to the world around me. Everything was centered around my actions and behaviors. We were guided by what we saw and what we were told to do. I recall there was an awful lot of 'telling' me what to do.

Here we are spinning around on a planet within this vast universe. I mean think about it. Really think. We are, with the help of gravity, spinning on a planet within a vast galaxy that is infinite. That's crazy. That certainly puts things into perspective, wouldn't you think? And, yet, we go about our lives, some really struggling, trying to make ends meet. Others worry, worrying about things that are out of their control. I know when I start whirling in my brain, worrying about things not in my control, I have to stop myself and say *enough*.

Did you know that we make 35,000 decisions a day? A day! This doesn't include the other 35,000+ thoughts we have about other things. So, I ask you--in any of that time are you thinking about *who you are?* -- probably not. Yet, I'm sure you've said to yourself at one point in your life, *What the hell am I doing in my life?* If this sounds familiar, then consider going back to the fundamental question of *Who are you?* It's worth exploring.

If you can indulge me for a moment, I'd like to ask you a few questions that only you have the answers to:

- What motivates you?

- What sort of temperament do you have?

- How would you describe your personality?

- What environment do you thrive in?

- If money were no object, what would you be doing?

- Whom do you like to hang out with?

- What gives you energy? What excites you?

- What depletes you?

- What's your philosophy on life?

- What values hold true for you?

- What is your own personal mission statement?

- If you were a brand, what would it be?

- Are you creative, analytical, quiet, high energy, nervous, anxious, happy, easy going, wired, uptight, etc.?

- Describe a perfect day.

- Describe your perfect living situation.

You get where I'm going with this. It takes some concerted effort and focused time to get to the bottom of, you. Once discovered, you'll have a much better idea as to how you want to live and be in this world. The clearer you are, the better you can visualize the connection between you and what you want and, as a result, you can help yourself to realize all the actions required to make it happen. It's not rocket science. It's taking the time to want to discover all the great things about yourself.

One thing we need to understand is that what we may have been drawn to when we were young will probably have changed. We may not be interested in the same things because we've grown as human beings. We've evolved and continue to evolve. As we learn, we discover more things about ourselves. As we move through various stages of our lives, we also gravitate toward different things. That's what makes us so fascinating. However, the essence of you, your

Be Your Truth

morals and values are pretty solid unless, of course, something has shifted in you.

## To Be Your Truth:
Let's go. Who are you? Take the time to answer the questions above. Sit with your responses for a while. Revisit them. Get as true to your heart as you can. Be honest. Be your truth.

Amy Goldberg

# I Know What's Holding You Back

There have been lots of books written about what's holding you back, how to succeed, how to get unstuck, and, yet, none of these will prove helpful to you IF you're not willing to take action. It must start with you. As they say, *You can lead a horse to water, but you can't make it drink.* It has to start with the desire to shift your mindset. The desire to start diving into all the things that give you energy. And, yet, what's it going to take? What's it really going to take for you to start making a difference in your life, to start shifting your mindset toward serving you better? You can read, listen, talk, experience, attend, consume things until you're blue in the face. Yet, it all adds up to zip if you don't take action.

**First you need to know what's holding you back.** Did you know that we all have a primitive part of our brain called the reptilian brain or amygdala? It's the part of the brain that warns us of danger, holds fear, resistance, anger, and negativity. It's the part of the brain that keeps you from succeeding. The amygdala is responsible for your fight or flight response. It wants to control your life from keeping you away from trying anything risky or new. It's the part of the brain that always has a Plan B. It questions everything. It thinks that your new idea will get you fired or bankrupt, that a new endeavor will ruin your life. It's telling you to shut up and stay in your comfort zone; do what you're told; don't rock the boat-- ever.

The amygdala (reptilian brain as it's also called) is the oldest part of the brain, and it's hardwired to take over whenever it senses danger. It doesn't, however, mean that you can't beat it. But first you need to recognize the reptilian brain tactics.

Here are some ways that the reptilian brain can sabotage you. It does it through:

Procrastinating
Being Overly Critical
Inventing Anxiety
Obsessing Over Details
Making Excuses

Now that you know the signs, how do you fight the reptilian brain?

**Here's how:** Allow yourself to:

Have Bad Ideas
Don't Make A Plan B
Train Yourself To Act The Opposite Of Your Reptilian Brain
Treat Failure As A Learning Experience. Embrace It
Don't Make Excuses. Show Up On Time-- Every Time.

When you change your perspective, it'll become easier for you to fight and win those battles that have kept you stuck. Trust me. Your reptilian brain will keep pushing you, and, yet, as you start to squash the noise from your reptilian brain, it will gradually become quieter and, eventually, a whisper. The most important thing is for you to start taking action. Every time your reptilian brain wants to hold you back, resist. Fight back by taking action. Watch. Soon you'll feel empowered that you're not listening to your reptilian brain whose only job is to hold you back. Take back your power.

## To Be Your Truth:

Practice often and allow yourself to take action. Go ahead and have those bad ideas; Don't make a Plan B; Train yourself to act the opposite of your reptilian brain; Treat failure as a learning experience. Embrace It; Don't make excuses. Show up on time-- Every time.

# When Life Disappoints You

When life gives you disappointments, it can turn your world upside down. I don't think we're actually equipped to handle setbacks and disappointments. If we were, then I think we would handle them better and/or differently. Why is it that every time you're disappointed, it seems as if it's happening to you for the first time? You seem to have the same unbelieving reaction to it.

Sure, if you never experienced disappointment, then you wouldn't know what the 'highs' in your life would feel like. I don't know about you, but I'd be just fine without ever having to be disappointed again or, at the very least, 'feel' the disappointment. I think it's time to take a different approach. At least, I need to.

What if you didn't 'feel' the disappointment? What if when you were faced with an answer or a circumstance that you weren't all that crazy about, you 'smiled' – actually and physically smiled? What would that 'feel' like? Your brain would now interpret that smile as *Hey, this is exciting!!! Obviously, I'm not on the right path, or I need to change my approach the next time. This is a GREAT learning experience. Bring it on baby. It's ALL good.*

Could you do that? Would you be able to do that? Of course, you could and would if you knew it would prove more healthful to you. Or would you? Why is it that you'd rather take the impulsive approach?

You do it every time you react to something. For example, you eat something knowing that it isn't good for you. You want to move from something and, yet, you stay stuck, unhappy, and uninspired. Why? -- because it seems a lot easier. It's the same thing as living your life on autopilot. What's the difference? The difference is your life would be a lot better, a lot happier, a lot healthier if you took a different approach. When you adopt a shift in your mindset that you've planned out or already know how you're going to handle disappointment, then it makes for a much better outcome.

It's the same thing as if you were sick with the flu. You're not yourself. You're lethargic. You have no energy. You're dragging yourself around-- if you can get yourself out of bed. It's the same thing. When you've shifted your mindset, it's as if you're 'well' again. You're not dragging your doubting, limiting beliefs and anticipatory feeling of being disappointed around with you. If every time you shifted any kind of disappointment into a positive learning experience, an experience that would otherwise not have happened, you will, over time, build resiliency, gain strength, lose the fear of failure, make better decisions, take further action, fight your fears, try more things, and experience a lot more in your life. That's a lot of great outcomes!

If and when you're faced with your next disappointment, try smiling--really smile. Then, feel what happens. Don't react. Sit with the feeling as you're still smiling. I'm not suggesting that you mask the lousy feeling of disappointment – go ahead and acknowledge it, but only AFTER you smile first. The first time you try this you may be smiling a lot longer than you expect to 'feel' the positive vibe. That's expected. After a while, disappointment will get less and less because you're reacting to it differently. Bring life on. Keep smiling.

## To Be Your Truth:

Practice smiling--often. It may seem forced at first, and, yet, you will feel how your disposition changes. Your energy will begin to feel elevated.

Amy Goldberg

# People Don't Get You.

One thing I do know--people will always want to change you. Even if they tell you they don't, it's probably not true. They really do.

***Why?*** -- because they want you to bend to their personality, their temperament, their own style, maybe even their own need for drama. I really have no idea. For some reason, I do feel that it makes others feel better about themselves. It 'normalizes' them. And, yet, here's the thing. There's no such thing as 'normal.' We want to define ourselves by terms and words that may make us 'feel' better, and, yet, it may be making us feel worse! Look. I get it. We're all trying to connect, to get closer. However, I know that as soon as someone says to me, *You're different* or *You haven't been the same lately* or *You know, when you say this or that* ... or *Stop saying* ...( you get where I'm going with this), then someone wants to morph you into something and/or figure you out through their eyes (not yours).

I don't feel I need to explain why I'm feeling a certain way unless, of course, I want to talk about it. Every day we are different people whether we know it or not. We have a different perspective.

## Be Your Truth

Every time we learn something, experience something new, we're different. We're growing all the time or, at least, I hope so. Have you ever noticed how many people offer their opinion when you haven't asked for it? If you ask someone if everything is OK and they reply *yes,* then I hope the person would leave it at that. Do they?

When someone persists in knowing what's up, then the conversation is shifted to them. Have you ever felt that you now need to reassure them that you're not *feeling different?* 'So now you're simply trying to appease them – that's ridiculous. It takes time to learn about ourselves. When someone projects their observations onto us, then it can throw us off.

I feel that people rush into getting to know another person rather than taking the time to understand better what makes each of us tick. Think about it. No two people are the same. So, when someone doesn't 'get you' then you can understand why. You're one of a kind. *That's profound.* We join tribes, communities, groups in order to feel more connected to like-minded people. We're social beings. However, I encourage you not to morph into someone else's idea of you. Bring yourself wherever you go. Enhance your involvement. Bring your energy and insight.

The one thing I would like to reassure you with is that it's OK that people may not get you or understand you. You don't need to prove anything to anyone other than yourself. I'm not sure you really believe that. As imperfect as we all are, we need to be perfectly OK with that. The imperfections that we have allow us to be more compassionate human beings. When people don't get you, that's OK. It's not about you, anyway. It's about them. So, the next time someone states something about you and you don't want to invite any further conversation around it, say, *That's an interesting perspective* or *That's interesting,* and leave it at that. *Go be YOU!*

## To Be Your Truth:

When you become more in tune with your truth, you won't worry about what others have to say. Be kind and, yet, don't morph into something that you're not.

## What's It All About?

We say *We're only human,* as if it excuses everything in our life that is real. What does that even mean, anyway? It means that we make mistakes. We fail. Rather than say *I screwed up* or something similar that denotes that we may have goofed up, we say that we're only human. I believe this has to do with our fragile minds being brainwashed at a young age not to screw up or there will be consequences. Even if you were brought up by wonderfully supportive parents or guardians, someone, anyone in your life that you've encountered that says something negative, it will hit you like a ton of bricks and that *'screw-up'* comment will be magnified-- guaranteed.

It's incredible how we are more attached to the negative aspects in our life than the things that are going well for us. Ah, to be human. Or is it? Why don't most of us have the fortitude and/or gumption to move past the negative and into our 'zone,' our 'sweet spot?' Does it seem too easy for us? Are we convinced that the other shoe will drop in our lives and that we're destined to lead a challenging life? I think yes-- or, at the very least, maybe.

How would life play out for us if we only led by our heart and not by our thoughts? Would there be mayhem? Would you start to *tell it like it is?* Would you tell your truth? Could we run an experiment like Jim Carey's character did in the movie "Liar, Liar" in which he couldn't tell a lie for an entire week – yes, a week. Are you laughing or crying right now? Would you be willing to try?

A flush of red just passed over my face as I quickly recall a meeting I had yesterday when a woman whom I'm becoming friends with expressed a keen interest in working together. We've brainstormed on a number of ideas and have landed on trying something. However, and this is a BIG red flag for me, she wants to collaborate, and, yet, she starts to throw around a lot of "I's" and "me's." saying *This is the way I want it* and *I don't want this, or that, or the other thing.* You get my drift? Hmmmm, the definition of the word 'collaboration' had just taken on a whole new meaning.

It's one who monopolizes the conversation. It's all about him or her. There is no conversation because, in fact, it's all about that person. In this case, it's about how great this person is. She can do no wrong. So, while I'm strongly criticizing this person (how horrible of me), imagine IF this were the week when I didn't lie. I would need to decline graciously, wanting to 'collaborate.' I would need to 'take a pass.' Why does that seem difficult? It shouldn't be. My truth would have the answers. I would be setting healthy boundaries.

## To Be Your Truth:

Being true to yourself; living your truth eliminates the *"maybes"* to get to *"yes"* and *"no"* with greater ease.

Amy Goldberg

## Good & Bad Days

If you know anything about yourself, you'd know that you display many emotions and feelings in any given day. Although some may pride themselves on hitting the ground day after day even keeled, it's just not the case. Our brains are a complicated matter. If you read any of the theories and research around our thoughts, then you'll also know that *"we are not our thoughts."* And if we're not our thoughts, then who are we? Someone is speaking to us. Who is it? And why is it spewing self-destructive thoughts -- thoughts, of self-doubt and limiting beliefs?

On the flip side, why are your thoughts also reeling a false sense of who you are? I believe that it's through our experiences, learnings, and interest in growing and developing as human beings that you start to decipher the noise in your head. You owe it to yourself to be able to tap into what's really going on.

Have you ever experienced over the course of a week, maybe a month, waking up and already being in a certain frame of mind? For example, Mondays for me have a 'feel,' a crappy feel. This is something that I have struggled with since my grade school years. It has nothing to do with my set up of the day. I could have a lot of great things planned and, yet, I still feel the doom and gloom that hovers over me on Monday. I say *snap out of it*. And, yet, the feeling remains. I'm working on it. This is definitely a work in progress. When Tuesday comes, at least for me, it's a whole different feel. Why?

Here's what I know. When I set up my day (apart from Monday) and I've planned out what I want to accomplish, I know I'm a lot happier. For example, every morning I know that I need to exercise. It sets me up. It spikes my brain. It shakes out the cobwebs. I also know that each day I need flexibility to accomplish what I need to do. As an entrepreneur and fierce believer in doing things that excite me (as much as I can) although I'm still working on it, I have come to know what works for me and what doesn't. I've honed it over time. The clearer I am with myself, the happier I become. It's when I settle, am complacent, that it messes me up.

Every single one of us will have a range of emotions throughout our day--some good, some great, others downright bad, and everything in between--guaranteed, no matter how 'joyful' you are. It's the *Life is what happens when you're out making other plans* (John Lennon) that can take over.

As a matter of fact, I believe that life happens for you. You need to learn to be adaptable, nibble, flexible, whatever you call it, so that you're better able to handle whatever comes your way. I know that when I lead with my heart and not with my head or, especially, not with my ego, wow, it's powerful. For sure, I'm happier. For sure, my heart feels full and open. It's when I get into my head and second guess what I'm doing or trying to do is when all hell breaks loose.

What I can offer you is a better understanding of yourself--a self that hovers over this planet looking for and trying out new things that excite you and give you energy. We all must strive for that. If we don't, we leave this world with regrets, regrets that we didn't take the time to experience more things, regrets that we didn't connect with more hearts and souls, regrets that we didn't lead with our heart.

So many people struggle, struggle to lead with their voice. Maybe you don't even know what your voice sounds like? Maybe it's being drowned out by external influences and people who don't encourage you or lift you up? Yes, as I always say, *It starts with you*, and, yet, in starting with you, you need to decide whom you want to surround yourself with. What do you want to be doing that gives you energy?

No matter what the inspirational, motivational leaders, speakers, and books say, you are not going to be in pure bliss all the time unless you've isolated yourself from the world, and, even then, as social creatures, you'll suffer. Know that whatever kind of day you decide to have, you have control over the choices that you make. When you're feeling bad, do the opposite of how you feel. Rather than stay in and cram a boat load of junk food into your body, call a friend and do something active. Get those endorphins pumping. Get yourself into a mastermind group in which you're brainstorming and tackling what it is that you want to accomplish. Seek support. Ask for what you need.

Be Your Truth

You may not always get it, and, yet, ask anyway. If you don't, then the answer is FOR SURE no. What kind of day do you want to have?

## To Be Your Truth:

Decide first thing every morning what kind of day you want. Life will throw you curveballs, and, yet, if you position your mind to show up the way you want to perceive things, watch what happens. You'll respond differently-- every time.

Amy Goldberg

# Loneliness is a Lonely Word

Loneliness is a word that elicits all kinds of emotions. It's that one word that has you feeling before thinking. I'm fascinated by word association. Being alone isn't the same as being lonely, nor is being lonely the same as loneliness. And, yet, loneliness can be a trigger to something long past and have little to do with how we feel today. I equate this to the smells I experienced when traveling around the world. It brings back a flood of memories both pleasant, odd, and foreign to me. That's called olfactory memory.

I was running with a friend when she asked, *What were the 3 times in your life that were most profound for you? What were the turning points?* As we talked, she noted that for her it was when she was 6 months and 3 years old when she experienced feeling abandoned and unloved. To this day, despite her brilliance, her struggle has been to feel connected and wanted. As a result, she tends to overcompensate by bending over backwards to help others. In addition, she says yes to things even when it's not the best fit for her. She loves the 'high' of being wanted, needed, and accepted. I get it. So, you see, we're fighting with our limiting beliefs and self-sabotaging thoughts all the while trying to overcome and/or come to terms with our demons-- our hurt feelings.

Life is a journey, a confusing, messed-up, roller coaster of a ride that, if you are not careful, can have you spiraling. We're all just trying to figure it out moment by moment. When you feel lonely, you may be one that tends to isolate yourself and cut yourself off from the world.

I know when I'm feeling lonely, I need to incorporate a few strategies. The first is to recognize that I'm feeling lonely and then start to open myself up to taking a more active role in life.

I'd like to offer these tools to help ease the loneliness you may be feeling. I know this helps me:

**Gather your thoughts** and acknowledge where your barriers are

**Turn loneliness into an ally**. Practice opening into it. Say *Bring it on,* and then see what happens. See what comes up for you?

**Get curious.** Open up your wide-angle view and embrace what's going on in the world. When you're out for a walk, rather than close yourself off, embrace the world. Shift your body language. Keep your chest open and walk tall. Be on a mission to experience more.

Most important, be present. It sounds so simple, and, yet, it's really difficult for a lot of us. We tend to live either in the past or project into the future. Know that all we have is right now. Own it. Loneliness is a state of mind. We have a choice to reset our mind. It takes work. And, yet, it's worth it. Start embracing where you are and what you're doing. If it's not working for you, start taking action toward making some changes. You have one life and many emotions. Pick the ones that work for you. Embrace the ones that suck and make them your friends. Eventually, you'll find that all of these feelings that you're having are temporary. The sun WILL come out …..

## To Be Your Truth:
In discovering your truth, you will also discover that the feeling of loneliness helps you to become a more resilient human being. I encourage you to try the steps listed above whenever you may need to.

# The Pivot

I can honestly say that I didn't really see it coming until, I did. I felt it both emotionally and physically. Not intellectually. Not then.

*Have you ever noticed that we're the last to know anything about ourselves?* The last to learn. To discover. To trust— ourselves. I was not the exception.

My turning point or pivot as I like to refer to it, evolved. It evolved because I wasn't aware of, nor was listening at the time to my instincts, my gut, my truth until it finally **SCREAMED** at me from deep within. *"WHAT ARE YOU DOING? KNOCK IT OFF. HEAR ME. FOR F\*CK SAKES."*

This pivot eventually showed me my strength, my resiliency, and what was really important to me. And yet …. it took years.

I realize that my pattern. My stress-appeaser was to run. Run both physically and emotionally. It started when I decided to travel around the world when I was younger. I was gone for just shy of 3 years. I thought I was leaving for my need to explore and experience the world. Upon further reflection, what I was really doing was running away. Running away from myself. As Jon Kabat-Zinn said in his book; *"Wherever you go there you are."* It turns out, it's not so obvious.

The reason why this pattern wasn't so obvious was because it created incredible experiences, life adventures, and wonderful business opportunities for me. Combined with my entrepreneurial spirit, it also caused havoc. It also overshadowed my understanding of how to trust what it was that I needed. I constantly questioned, where I fit in. What was I doing, and why? Always fighting my truth. Every step of the way.

I was leading my life through the eyes of others and not that of my own. I had one toe in, everything. Spinning for the sake of feeling worthwhile. Knowing that I was miserable. Burnt out. Bummed out. When you're seeking recognition, it's emotionally exhausting. It also makes you feel small and angry. And more importantly, it effects your health. The kicker for me was that I had always known that I was better than that. Better than my limiting beliefs. My self-doubt. The bulls*t I created in my mind. All the while, I was suppressing a lot of my curiosity, optimism, fun, creative, and loving self. What was that all about?

Ironically, I realized that by running I was able to breathe. I was looking outwardly for the answers. Running resolved that for me — temporarily.

And then, it hit me. I stopped dead in my tracks. It wasn't until the exhaustion caught up with me that I reflected upon the answers. I needed to stop looking outside myself to find my breath. What I needed was to look within. I needed to breathe from within.

*This was my pivot.* It was that day that I took action. I looked for strategies and methods that would bring me closer to myself. I started deep breathing exercises; meditation training; reading more about mindset and awareness. I balanced my exercise routine so that it wouldn't deplete me; it would give me more energy.

By having strategies that I could tap into, at any time, lifted the trust within myself. It created a stronger understanding of my "zone of genius," so wonderfully coined by; Gay Hendricks in his book "The Big Leap."

Today, I lead a healthy more prioritized life whereby I'm able to help accelerate other people's lives. There's nothing more satisfying then to be able to lift others – to help other's rise. This can truly only take place when you decide that it has to start with you – first.

## To Be Your Truth:

Think back to when you first pivoted in your life. What did you learn about yourself? What was revealed to you? Are you a better person because of it? Life pivots help you to stay on a track. It doesn't mean it has to be on the same track.

# PART 2

# Is It Just Me?

Here's the part where we determine if we are, in fact, aligned with who we think we are. Do our actions reflect us? The essence of who we are. This is where we need to dive into our reality and ask the hard question: *Am I living my truth? Or am I full of sh\*t. And if I'm full of sh\*t then am I ok with living THAT truth?*

# Is It Just Me?

*This is where the doubt begins.*

I was convinced at a young age that I was the only one on this planet that saw things completely differently— the way we live our lives, the way we connect with others or avoid others; our unhealthy egos, how we treat ourselves, what's decided for us when we're born, our behavior toward others, our lack of self-awareness. Do you get where I'm going with this?

It was exhausting being young and in this world with the expectation that I needed to create myself which, in itself, would be incredibly exciting. However, the first many, many years I was way too busy reprogramming what I absorbed, learned, and believed to be true when I was too young to decide for myself. It was crushing for me to understand that a lot of things I was learning were mostly bullshit. I was so confused.

During the first part of my life, I had little guidance. I did things that sounded good. I was that *Sure sounds good* person that was, in fact, floundering. If I had actually listened to myself, I would have been on a whole different journey. Wait a minute-- maybe not. It was probably that very journey that led me to trust myself, that led me to become a better person, that led me to understand better who I was and what I was capable of doing.

I love this quote: *As you start to walk on the way, the way appears* by Rumi who was a 13th century scholar and poet. Basically, what he's saying is (or, at least, this is my interpretation) *Have faith and believe the dots will connect.* Wouldn't it be great if that really were how we lived our lives? There would be no stress, no worries. Our fears and doubts would disappear. We would trust wholeheartedly that it will all work out. So, why am I telling you this? – because we don't live our lives like that at all. In fact, we probably have never lived our lives like that. And it started at the age of 3 or 4 when an adult asked us, *What do you want to be when you grow up?* It's now in our brain. We're sponges, absorbing everything that is told to us.

Fast forward and depending upon our life conditions, we're expected at the age of 16 or 17 to decide what we want to be doing with the rest of our lives. We need to decide, or worse, someone decides for us: *Do I continue with formal education? Learn a trade? Get a Job. Start or go into a business? Maybe take a year off before deciding anything.* Some are just trying to survive day to day. It's tough and all so confusing. Maybe you were that kid at age 3 or 4 who knew exactly what you wanted to be when you grew up. Fantastic, but guess what? You, too, will experience challenges, disappointments, scary moments, uncertainty. We all do. No one goes unscathed.

One interview that is burned in my brain was one with a young woman who created a YouTube series. She interviewed women from varied professions to find out what the secrets to their success and life were.

This young woman was in Grade 11 at the time. She went to an all girls' private school. As we were talking, she said, *The biggest source of stress and anxiety for herself and her peers was getting into the right college or university.* She went on to say that *Once they were accepted into the 'right' school, they were so relieved.* Apart from the obvious, I asked her why? She said, *Most of the girls are so relieved because they consider getting into the right school their final destination.* I kid you not – their final destination.

Here are a few things I gleaned from this conversation. I mentioned private school because even in schools where one would think that you'd have the tools that you needed to position yourself for your life journey, you still have the one and only thing hovering in the minds of young women. They are expected to enter the 'right' school. It's ingrained in their minds. This mindset comes with its own challenges. But when you're locked-on and heading in the direction you think you should be going; you tend to suppress your curiosity and intuition. You have blinders on which means you could be diverting your attention to clues that could be taking you in the direction of discovering what you truly love to do or want to be doing.

As well, it also hinders your ability to hone your skills such as resiliency, adaptability, flexibility, and thinking strategically because the reality of what you study in school and the career path that you take are very different. You're not taught that. And, then, as a constant reminder, society wants to know ALL THE TIME what school you went to and what do you do for a living. We're rarely asked, *What do you like to do? What gives you energy?* What happens is if you don't give the answer that people want to hear, they disengage, and you start to feel inadequate and start doubting yourself, saying, *What's wrong with me? I don't know what I want. I don't fit this mold.* This takes you further and further away from trusting yourself, from your journey and believing that the dots will connect because all of your actions, beliefs, and behaviors don't align at all with this truth.

Imagine how different life would be for you if you recognized that everything that you've done so far is for you to learn and grow as a human being, knowing that if you kept repeating the same mistakes over and over again rather than evolving, then you haven't quite learned from those mistakes in order to move on. You do eventually evolve if you listen for it. And, yet, despite all of this, today, right here, right now, I'm here to say that you are exactly where you need to be.

What if everything that you've done up until this point in your life was supposed to have happened, was supposed to have made sense, and that it was revealing to you that the dots will connect? Could it be that you're simply not listening to the signs, the clues, your energy around what it is that is guiding you--ALL OF IT--the struggles, the failures, the learnings, the successes?

Have you ever played the game in which someone hides something in a room, and you have to look for it? The ONLY clue that they give you is to say, *You're getting warmer, warmer, hotter, OR cold, colder, etc.* What if all along your life detector, because you have one, was doing the EXACT same thing for you? You know the feeling when you knew that a new role, career path, activity or relationship just didn't feel right. You had no energy around it. However, you found renewed energy when you found the things you love, the things that give you energy.

STOP FIGHTING IT. Let go.

In listening for clues, your energy tells you a lot about yourself-- what you gravitate toward--what interests you. It doesn't even need to be decisive. It's finding things that keep your interest. It's trying things out to see if you like it. IF you listened hard enough, you would discover all the things that connect you to your journey. If, however, you don't listen and follow others or get derailed, it's because you weren't listening. Those "warmer, warmer" moments when you're trying and doing things, when time stands still because you're in the moment and enjoying what you're doing – those are DOTS. Those are the things you need to be doing more of.

If I listened to people's opinions of how I *should* have been leading my life, 90% of what I've done so far in my life would never have happened. Interestingly, every time I did something that didn't sit well with me, I was miserable. Following someone else's goals and desires and not my own when there was little to no alignment was brutal. Being miserable made me more grateful. The choices I was making, good or terrible, were actually helping me because I finally had to wake up and listen.

If you're going through life with expectations that don't align with who you are and your unique energy, then you're missing out on what could be. You are NOT floundering in life. You are just NOT listening to yourself or, worse, much worse, you're afraid. Fear paralyzes us. We are afraid because we don't trust ourselves enough.

Think about it this way-- failing to get your perceived goal (typically what others expect of you) sometimes gets you to your destiny. That's powerful. This means that the things that don't work out for you, when you're disappointed, actually bring you closer to your destiny. You must have the courage to follow your heart and intuition. They somehow already know what you truly want to 'be.' Everything else, all the other stuff, becomes secondary.

Think of your life as a 'connect the dots drawing.' It's your story unfolding. You know in the coloring books where they have a drawing that you can't quite make out? It's fuzzy, and then you start to connect the dots. The dots will start to reveal the image. That's your life if you were to listen to it. Each dot represents an experience, a journey, an event, a career move, a connection, a moment in time where you possibly felt inspired, energized. Those are the dots that you want to keep connecting. All the other stuff was the learnings, failures, moments that have you recognize that you need to bring yourself back to your energy.

So how do you know you're on the right path? How do you trust that *As you walk on the way, the way appears?*

Try this:

## **An Exercise:**

**Start an energy log.** Get a notebook. I say notebook because research shows that by writing things down (rather than typing), we stimulate different parts of our brain, and we are better able to capture and retain more information when we put pen to paper. In your notebook draw a line down the middle of the page. On one side write down the word Energy at the top of the page. On the other side, write down the word Depleted on the top of the page.

**Every day for 2 weeks**, with your notebook in hand, start to keep a log of how you're feeling, what kind of energy you have around what you're doing. Do you have energy, or do you feel depleted? This applies to activities that you are doing--your work, your hobbies, the food you eat, how you wake up in the morning, the people you hang out with. Jot it all down. Soon you will start to see patterns.

If you are seeing over time, day to day, that you are more depleted than energized, guess what? You need to make some changes. You need to ask yourself, "What's holding me back? What am I afraid of? What do I need to ask for in order to get to where I'm going?" If you're still not sure how to connect the dots in your life, try things. Experience things. The more you experience, the more you have to offer. I'm going to add on to that. *The more you experience, the more you have to offer YOURSELF.* Stay curious. Look for things around you that elevate your energy.

*You can't see the dots going forward; you can only see them looking backwards.* Steve Jobs (creator & founder of Apple) said that.

This means you need to trust your gut, karma, destiny, your intuition, whatever that is for you. No one is like you. You have talents that are uniquely yours.

Life is short. Don't lose faith. Don't settle. You matter. You've got to find and do what you love. Think about it like this: Look at your life so far and think about every time you got excited. Those are dots. Those dots reveal a common thread. That's what you should focus on. You've come too far to give up on who you are. Believe the dots will connect.

## To Be Your Truth:

For 2 weeks keep an energy log. Follow the exercise above. It works!

# A Real Jerk

*And now we need to show up in the world with these jerks?*

And here lie the inconsistencies of your truth. I am positive that you are not walking the walk IF you think you're leading with your authentic self unless, of course, your truth is that you're a jerk. But I digress. Here's where I merge off a bit into something that I observed.

My friend said, *What? You, Amy, are writing about jerks? You, who always has a smile on her face, a happy-go-lucky person who is one of the most positive (annoyingly so) people I know on this planet? What gives?"*

After I laughed at my friend's comment, I said, *Isn't it a sad state of affairs when someone like me experiences the dark, nasty and narcissistic weight of people looming in my creative, joyful space?* And, yes, I'm ticked off despite the fact that I'm quite capable of shifting almost any conversation to reflect a more upbeat tone, adding an element of humor, I'm finding I have to work harder, more often, to maintain this frame of mind. I ask you, *How can so many people wake up with such crappy dispositions?* Jerks can trigger anxiety, depression, sleep problems, high blood pressure, and poor relationships with their colleagues, families, and partners. And for what? -- so that the world can lean into their evil, maniacal tendencies. I won't have it, nor should you.

But I digress. What triggered my own need to write this? One aspect of my work apart from writing, being a well-being entrepreneur, curating courses, and helping others find more effective strategies to lead happier lives, is being invited to speak at various industry events. I love it-- for the most part. I have, and I kid you not, received emails in which the event organizer will type the event date/time and a request for a speaker and nothing else. And, so, the email trail begins-- back and forth with what feels like grunts from the other end. It's as if the person is saying, *I'm leading with my ego. I have nothing better to do than to be unkind or unhelpful trying to get what I need.* In fact, it feels as if they couldn't care less. Maybe they don't. So, the first thing I do is, of course, not play into it. Yes, I believe in leading with kindness. Also, I do have a 'How to Deal With Jerks' playbook which lists a few of the following that do prove helpful. Are you ready?

## *How To Deal With Jerks Playbook*

**1. Don't judge.** Maybe they're having a bad day. There are relationship challenges (I can see why – whoops, don't judge). Maybe they're hungry. All these things play into one's mood. Give the benefit of the doubt. Take this into consideration. We're all human. Show empathy. *until it doesn't work, and you realize that ....*

**2. They Really Are A Jerk** Then, if you can't do anything about the situation after trying to resolve any miscommunication or any given situation, then understand, at the end of the day 'It's not worth it.' Please note: If you're in a work environment in which office politics and backstabbing are the norm, it's very likely you're not going to change the culture unless you have backing. It's time to consider alternatives for yourself.

*Then you need to step up and ....*

**3. Hold Your Ground** Remember jerks are everywhere. When it comes to conflicts, let the other person know how you feel about a situation. No matter how big of a jerk someone is, it's very difficult to disagree with feelings. You also need to remember that you don't want to turn into a jerk yourself. So, you're not blaming, you're explaining the situation. In no way, however, should you feel powerless in your life. You need to stand up for yourself with dignity and pride.

Regardless of the results of your encounters with jerks, if you decide to say no to them, you will remain in control of who you are-- and your truth.

*This is your life. Own it.*

## To Be Your Truth:

You can't be a jerk if you become your truth. Something's going on. The jerk in you is a deep-seated memory or experience from some point in your life. Take the time to figure it out. Reach into your anger. This is typically fear-based. Start there. If you're on the receiving end of a jerk, I suggest you carry the ***How To Deal With Jerks*** playbook around with you.

## Are You Sure You Mean To Say Smart?

*"It's not that I'm so smart, I just stay with problems longer."* – Albert Einstein

This is where you lose sight of your own truth. This is where you need to get real with yourself and speak your truth. Yes, I'm still on a tangent, and, yet, I thought I would share one more shift in thinking before we get back to you and your fabulousness. Actually, however, it does relate directly to your sense of self and how you see yourself and others, perhaps indirectly drawing upon your own insecurities and your misalignment to what you really mean and want.

Consider this if you will. How did 'we' get to a place where we find it necessary to proclaim always, what seems like <u>every single time,</u> after meeting someone how smart he or she is? Listen for it the next time someone describes someone whom they've met. Are we even describing the person accurately? Are you telling me that everyone is that smart? That would be

great if that were the case. However, I doubt that very much, given the grim political climate. OK, I'm not going there. The reason why I'm drawing attention to this is because we tend to misuse the word or sentiment when best describing someone. Ultimately and in turn, this misuse has most likely watered down the true meaning of what being 'smart' really is. I'd even go so far as to say that it does a disservice to those who are actually smart and intelligent people.

Furthermore, does being smart and intelligent mean the same thing? But I digress, and yet let's go there …Interestingly, we do tend to think of the words smart and intelligent to be interchangeable. However, there is a difference between the meanings and use of these words.

Being smart is an earned status, a trait a person can acquire. It's also defined by the ability to adapt, read a situation and apply the information. Intelligence, on the other hand, is a trait a person is born with. It's measurable (IQ test). Additionally, being smart has a practical component whereas intelligence, believe it or not, isn't always practical.

Having said that, I'd like to know what people mean when they say *smart*. It probably means that they're generalizing from a single instance in which the person knew something they didn't. It has been my experience that a number of my female friends when best describing the qualities they're looking for in their 'ideal' partner (no such thing) will say that he (in this case) has to be smart. What immediately comes to mind when I hear the 'list' with 'smart' topping the charts are *Poor guy. Oh, the pressure*!

I push forward for some clarity and say, *What do you mean by smart?* In fact, it's not about being smart at all. What I'm hearing is something entirely different. I proceed, *Go on. Well,* says my friend *he needs to be able to carry on a conversation, be financially secure, and interested in what I have to say.* Interpretation: He needs to be emotionally available, wealthy, and a good listener. Did you read 'smart' anywhere in that description?

What I'm trying to convey is that when you meet someone for 5 minutes and go away thinking/saying that she/he is 'smart,' it makes one believe that perhaps 'smart' isn't necessarily what you mean, which doesn't make you sound smart--which makes me sound smart-alecky, and

I don't want to end on a smart-alecky note. My attempt at sounding 'cute' doesn't always translate well onto paper.

Consider this if you will. When you're in conversation with people you meet for the first time, it's likely you'll glean some interesting tidbits, new information, thoughts, ideas, perhaps a different perspective. It may not necessarily be labelled as 'smart.' I think the real truth is that you're just so happy to have a conversation that doesn't involve texting that the first thing that comes to mind is the word smart.

## To Be Your Truth:

Take notice. The next time you say that another person is smart, which, of course, he or she could be, see why you're saying it. Is it because you're not feeling confident? You may be doubting yourself or insecurity is setting in. Or, hey, maybe that person IS simply smart. See what turns up for you.

Amy Goldberg

# But ...
## *We tell ourselves lies anyway*

It's time-- today-- right here--Right now--to stop making excuses for yourself. Our default mindset tends to be set on lazy mode. For some it takes all they can do to muster up enough energy to get the daily things done. Does this sound like you? No? Not at all? *I'm Gary Vaynerchuk on caffeine. Leave me alone.* For all those who are not Gary V on caffeine ... let's push on. What happens when it comes time for you, your needs, your desires, your goals and aspirations? I hear what you're thinking: *What are you talking about-- goals and aspirations? By the time the end of the day rolls around, I'm too exhausted to even think about me.*

That's why this is important. It's time for you to take control of your life and start to make things happen for yourself. Stop waiting for someone to come along and magically wave his or her wand. NO ONE is coming. Stop looking around. It's you--yes, you who has everything you need to take the first of many steps. Wasn't it you who first learned how to walk? No one did it for you. The same thing applies here. Taking ownership of your life starts with the understanding that you have choices. If your choices up until this point haven't been the best, then you need to recognize that you're enabling your poor decisions. Hard stop.

This usually comes with excuses. You're tired. You have no time. You'll do it tomorrow. You get where I'm going with this?

What's it going to take for you to get out of your own way and stop making excuses? What's it going to take for you to start owning your life and start taking action toward pushing yourself further? We live in a world of instant gratification. When we don't get it, we tend to give up. What happens then is that time goes by whether we're ready for it or not. One day you're going to realize that time just slipped through your fingers, and you'll stand there scratching your head wondering; *What the ....?* Even if you're that guy, Gary V, you're still saying it because time still moves way too fast.

Imagine if every day you did one thing that moved you toward your goals, goals that helped to build your confidence and move you to the next level. Stop sacrificing your goals and settling for autopilot. Your life and what brings you joy matter. That elusive happiness is within you to have. It truly is. Who said *Fear is not an option?* That person was right. Think about it. Apart from being chased by a saber-toothed tiger, when did fear serve you? It doesn't help you. It doesn't change the situation. Fear simply feeds an already chaotic situation and does nothing to solve it.

*Quit kicking yourself in the "butt" and get going.*

What are you waiting for?

## To Be Your Truth:
Do one thing that moves you in the direction of your truth, that truth being you and what you know to be true for yourself. IF you are not in a place that is aligned with who you are, do one thing to take action. Then keep going.

## Is Motivation Overrated?

*The biggest adventure you can take is to live the life of your dreams.* ~ Oprah Winfrey

*K*ick it into high gear. Don't hesitate when your instincts say 'Go.' Follow your energy around what excites you. It's that energy that will create the momentum when you need it most. When you want to give up, tap back into that energy. Remember why you started. Trust yourself. Keep it real for yourself. Don't worry about what others think. As a matter of fact, don't believe everything you tell yourself--you know, the negative self-doubts and insecurities that hold you back. Go be YOU whatever that looks like. Life is way too short for anything else.

Having just read the above, how do you feel? Does it do anything for you? Are you inspired? Are you saying *yes?* OR are you feeling irritated, annoyed, even anxious? Did you know that the way one thing motivates you is the way everything motivates you?

**Motivation** | noun | mo·ti·va·tion
"The reason or reasons one has for acting or behaving in a particular way"

When I talk about "It Starts With You" and walking the walk, this is you being you - only better. *Huh? What? That makes no sense.* Hear me out. When you get closer to your truth-- who you are and how you want to show up in your life, then you will be tapping into your authentic self. A way to take this one step further is to discover and build-on what motivates you, rather, what excites you. Once you know what excites you in life, then you will be able to take action which evolves into motivation. It's kind of ass backwards.

Why? --mostly because even when you discover what excites you, you still have to do the work. You need now to move into action. Our brain, the part that resists everything, gets in the way. It tells us all the reasons why we'd suck at something. The very definition of "motivation" tells us that we need to act or behave in a particular way. It's not easy. The key to motivation is purposeful action. So, what does that look like for you? What will drive you toward taking action toward your truth? This goes back to what excites you.

Intrinsic motivation, or the motivation to put effort into achieving personal fulfillment, tends to be far more rewarding than external motivation, when you're driven by external rewards such as money, power, status, or recognition. That stuff is fleeting if you're not truly jived by what you're doing.

When you feel like giving up (which you will, a lot), it'll be your truth that keeps you moving forward. So, is motivation overrated?

No, it's not. I'm going to suggest it's the way we think about things. If you're waiting to feel motivated to do something, it'll be a long time coming. If you know what excites you, start doing. Take action. Do something that moves the needle--every day.

Here's what I'm suggesting:

**Set a Goal.** Decide what you want and write it down.

**Visualize your Goal.** This works with athletes; it'll work for you, too. Imagine your goal to the detail. See it. Feel it. Hear it. Visualize the outcomes, what you want, who's with you. You get what I mean? Play it all out in your mind.

**Make a List.** Take pen to paper. List all the reasons why you want to accomplish this goal. It's easy to get off track. Writing down your goal pulls it all together.

**Break Down your goal into Achievable Actions.** It can be overwhelming trying to accomplish a goal when there is so much to do. Think of your goal in bite size pieces. Think of it this way: If you gulp the whole thing down at once, you're probably going to choke.

**Have a Strategy.** Life happens. Be prepared to be flexible. You may need to change course or shift gears. Keep the end goal in mind. Even if you have to hack out a new path, keep going.

**Seek Support.** Get the support that you need. Surround yourself with people better than yourself. Have the courage to be vulnerable. We all need guidance in one way or another.

**Be Prepared for Setbacks.** Guaranteed setbacks are going to happen. Guaranteed you'll feel like giving up. That's why it's so important to set a goal that you really want, that's going to bring you fulfillment. Setbacks actually make us stronger. Keep going.

**See the Big Picture.** Always remember your "Why." Why you're doing this. Keep visualizing your end goal. Gain strength from this.

## To Be Your Truth:

Once you become your truth you will start to move in the direction of what it is that you want. I'm suggesting that you start by following the steps above. You've got this.

# Let's Not Use The Word "Let"
*And now we're needing permission? WTF?*

I was reading an article the other day in which the writer was talking about work/life balance. He said that, in fact, it's not about balance. It's about 'fit.' I happen to agree with him. This same conversation, studies, research, and anything else related to work life balance has come up for what seems to be a lifetime. It first came up for me in the 90's when I disputed the notion, saying, *Isn't it about priorities rather than balance? People could go mad if they truly believed that they needed to find the holy grail of work/life balance. Does anyone agree with me here?* It fell on deaf ears. I'm not so sure we've truly moved on from this idea. I still see sessions, talks, and workshops on work life balance. But I digress. What does any of this have to do with what I'm writing about? I'm getting there!

### Let's Not Use The Word 'Let'

In the same article, the writer went on to talk about one's working style and how important it was to align with and ensure that one's work style fit with one's own style. In the same sentence he gave the example of how important it was to *work in a way that suits us.* For example, *Give me control over my time and space, and I'm amazed.* OK, great, I love it so far.

But ...This really irked me. In the same sentence as, and I'm paraphrasing, *Thankfully, some really smart companies are adapting to their employees' needs. They have core days when they let employees work from home or work how they like on, maybe, Monday and Friday. But on Tuesday, Wednesday, Thursday are in-office days where people can see one another.* Am I the only one that is picking up on the ridiculousness of this?

In this day and age, we're <u>still</u> actually treating people like morons! We're <u>still</u> saying *us and them*. We're <u>still</u> not trusting the people we hire. We <u>still</u> use language that contradicts itself. We're <u>still</u> not looking at individuals and how they work best. We're <u>still</u> not accessing human resources to help people actually be their amazing selves. *It's not rocket science.*

It's about honest conversations. It's about adults speaking with adults. It's about trust. Where did anyone get the idea that one should be so thankful that you're "letting" one do something or setting the exact same policies for everyone? Oh, no, there would be mayhem!!

Finally, and trust me, this IS the icing on the cake. The writer ends by saying, *Clearly both parties – workers and companies – benefit from the flexibility of allowing a work/life fit. Companies likely see improved productivity and a more engaged workforce.* And blah, blah, blah. There was more, but it was so poorly written that I stopped reading. I got the gist. Hope you do too.

Imagine if you empowered, enabled, embraced, and engaged people to do their best work in a way that best 'fit' their style (whatever that looked like), and then watched what would happen. I imagine, or rather I hope, that you 'had people' at value, mission, and vision when they first joined the organization. That's what they signed up for. They believed in you and your company when they were given the role. Now, enable them to do what they said they were going to do. If it doesn't work out, then part ways. Yes, it's expensive to recruit good people. But it's even more expensive if it doesn't work out. So, do it right the first time. Collaborate together to create the best-case scenario for both of you.

*Boom. Mike drop. Stepping off the stage.*

## To Be Your Truth:

When you are your truth, you will know your truth. You will have a clearer and more confident voice wherever you are. I cite the workplace because that's where a lot of us spend our time, whether an entrepreneur, owner, or employee. You should be able to flourish. Bring your best self to create. This includes being a fulltime stay-at-home mom or dad. Your interactions need to be authentic and true to yourself. Let go of "let." Just be and thrive.

Amy Goldberg

# Please. Stop. Networking

*How do you show up?*

Here we go again, and, yet, it's relatable. I'll ask the question anyway: *What does this have anything to do with you and how you should be leading your life, your truth?* Interestingly, and I've mentioned this a few times, and yet it's worth repeating; how you are in the world, how you show up, and how you communicate has to come from a place of who you are and how you want to be. Too often you are programmed. All of us are. We are told to be, act, do, and present ourselves in a cookie-cutter fashion.

A small example of this is when I hear about networking events or activities related to 'networking,' I cringe. It conjures up feelings that are forced, phony, programmed, robotic, insincere, lackluster, trying too hard, stiff, inauthentic ... you get my drift? This is not to be mistaken with Social Networking. That's a whole other story.

There are courses and workshops on *How to Network effectively*. I find, however, that there is always one missing key element to it--actually *connecting with people*. In my opinion, we're thinking about this the wrong way. No two people should be networking the same. I believe it's having a negative effect on us both personally and professionally.

From a personal aspect networking quite often is associated with induced stress and anxiety--the feeling of *being thrown to the lions.* Our fight or flight response kicks into high fear. That's not good. Yeah, yeah, I'm all for getting out of your comfort zone and being *comfortable with being uncomfortable.* And, yet, to me: *Forced conversations + Fear = Disaster*

In fact, let's STOP calling it networking right here and now. Let's create a new language. Let's put some breathing space around what you're doing in order to create a more positive and satisfying mindset, an empowering mindset. Let's take a more joyful approach. Set yourself up for success. Let's call it *building relationships.* How does that feel to you?

Here's the thing. I don't believe that building relationships should be forced--ever. Don't get me wrong. I'm all for 'gatherings,' but with the mindset of having the opportunity to meet new people and share ideas. I'll try to bring this all home for you. For the purpose of this story, I'm going to use the word 'Networking.' This is a perfect scenario in which networking was ridiculous (and humorous).

Recently I was at a LinkedIn local Meetup. I was invited by the organizer. We were going to meet up for breakfast the day before this event. However, plans changed. I now needed to be out of town. I thought this would be a perfect opportunity to put a face to a name and have a brief conversation. He knew I was coming. I walked into the building where the event was being held. It was a small venue. I purposely arrived early to connect with the organizer, which I did briefly-- very briefly. He walked toward me. I gave him a big smile thinking he recognized me. In fact, he was eyeballing a table and chair. He was sitting down to review what was on his phone. I went over and said, *Hello [name goes here], my name is Amy*. I put context around who I was. I didn't want to assume. He looked up for a second and said, *Hi*. I picked up that he was busy. He was reviewing his notes. I said, *I can see that you're busy. I'll leave you to it*. I then started to say I hope we can catch up later. Nope. He quickly dismissed me.

This. Was. A. Networking. Meetup. Priorities were a little askew.

OK, I get it. He was prepping. However, it was a small gathering which he's led hundreds of times before. He chose to prep rather than pause to connect briefly with me. Oh, did I mention that he brands himself as *It's ALL about connection?* [insert laugh track]

Putting ego aside, I proceeded to "Network." The word "Networking" was used about 15 times throughout the evening. The organizer encouraged everyone to network before the more formal part of the evening started. It felt like a game. Networkers start your timer. Ready. Set. Go. No, actually, it felt more like speed dating, and you know how those turn out... not well. It felt so forced. At one point I overheard a person giving an 'elevator pitch.' The person asked for a '*do over.*' I kid you not.

As the networking continued, I joined a small group of people that were gathered. They were all talking *at* one another, rather than *with* one another. Then this happened. Within this small group was a woman that was constantly looking at her phone that she had in her hand. She would ask the name of a person with whom she was speaking and then proceed to type on her phone. When it came to me, I started to strike up a conversation. After all, we were right there, in the room together, facing each other. Rather than speak with me, she asked my name and went right to her phone. I watched. She had the LinkedIn page open. She typed in my name in the search bar. She clicked 'connect.' You can't make this shit up. She had little interest in having a conversation. It was as if she were collecting people for the sake of collecting people. Needless to say, I DID NOT accept her LinkedIn invitation to CONNECT.

In hindsight, I wish I had pointed out what she was doing. I wish I had conveyed to her that her method was a sure-fire way to turn people off. And, yet, come to think of it, no one seemed bothered by it. Maybe they were like me using their internal voice, thinking, *You're an idiot.* It was as if this group had been taught or conditioned to network this way. You see …. the word 'Networking' makes people do this!

What happened to being yourself, to being genuine and authentic, to being curious, to connect and communicate in a meaningful way? What can you learn from this? If you replace the word or function of 'Networking' with building 'Relationships,' would that shift your thinking, your approach, the way in which you connect? A word of advice, if I may. Stop worrying about elevator pitches and introductions and start listening-- really listening. As you get to know people, it would seem more appropriate sharing or sending them relevant information or resources that you know would help them personally and/or professionally.

This may help:

**Three things to consider**

(Excerpted from J. Kelly Hoey author of "Build Your Dream Network") – Note: I'm making an exception with the word 'Network.' Her heart is in the right place.

- Networking is about enhancing your people skills. It's every human interaction from your smile in the elevator to your voicemail message. Forget "working the room" and insert more empathy into how you connect with colleagues every day.

- Network your expertise! Volunteer to mentor. Join an industry committee. Contribute to a company blog. 70% of career opportunities are attributed to word-of-mouth referrals. To advance your career, it's not simply who you know or what you know but who knows what you know.

- Avoid "groupthink" by expanding your network. Ensure you're connecting with people outside your professional field, social circle, age demographic, and geographic location

## To Be Your Truth:

Keep it real. To be your truth means that you don't need gimmicks, tricks, maneuvers, or anything else that's not your truth.

Amy Goldberg

# The WOW Factor
*Do you know what it is?*

Did you know that The Wow Factor is actually a thing? The definition states that *it's the distinctive appeal that an object, behavior or person has on others.* In other words, *it's an impressive display brought on by the experience of something or someone.* In knowing this, how would you go about getting the WOW factor IF you wanted it? Have you ever thought about it? I'm interested in knowing …. Have you ever thought about YOUR WOW Factor? Did you know that every single one of us has it? Yep.

In a world where one would think we were fully and wholeheartedly self-aware, the opposite is actually true. We're the least self-aware in so far as to say that we really don't understand who we are and what we're capable of. What's happened is that we've mistaken being self-aware with taking selfies. OK, I'm kidding. And, yet, and I'll keep repeating myself: it starts with you. How well do you know yourself?

*Knowing yourself is the beginning of all wisdom.* - Aristotle

How aware and conscious are you of your thoughts, actions, needs, desires, habits, strengths, weaknesses, emotions, values, and motivations?

**WARNING:** If you're coming from a place of ego, then you will not be able objectively and honestly to examine, assess, discover, evaluate and uncover your WOW factor unless, of course, you're the only one that sees it. In that case, I hate to be the bearer of bad news. You then need to go back to learning more about becoming self-aware.

If you're able to dig deep and identify your distinct and unique qualities that set you apart, (for example; your strengths, personality traits, interesting perspective, that sort of thing), you then may want to confer with your closest confidants whom you trust and respect for feedback. This helps to remove any preconceived bias that you may have of yourself. Mastery of self takes real work. We're mostly comfortable with our surface self unless, however, something happens to us, and we have to dig deeper. And, even then, we make a choice either to deal with the need to understand ourselves better or run the other way. In that case, it becomes avoidance and deflection. It's just the way we are. If, however, you've embraced the challenge really to understand yourself, then it's time to take what you know about yourself and combine it with your passion.

Passion: A strong liking or desire for or devotion to some activity, object, or concept.

Assuming you've figured out who you are, the next questions to ask yourself are: (and you should know the answers if you've done the 2-week exercise in this book) *What gives me energy? When does time stop for me when I'm involved in something that I like doing? What sparks me?*

Still not sure? Let's go deeper. Consider the following 3 questions:

1. What subject could I read 500 books about without getting bored?

2. What could I do for five years straight without getting paid?

3. What would I spend my time doing if I had complete financial independence to do anything?

*Anything that gets your blood racing is probably worth doing.* – Hunter S. Thompson

Once you've answered the above, start to list the jobs or tasks that you absolutely loathe. You should also have this list readily available from the previous exercise. You see, I'm on to you if you've been skimming this book. In doing this, you can easily weed out what you don't like. It's far easier to know what you don't like than it is to know what you do-- hence, the reason why we're revisiting this.

By now you're gaining further insight into who you are, your unique qualities, and what you enjoy doing. If, however, you need a little more to go by, I encourage you to try to visualize your best day. I didn't say 'perfect day' for a reason. There's truly no such thing as perfect. The word perfect in fact adds unnecessary pressure. It doesn't make anything easier. Research has shown that there's a strong correlation between what we see and what we do. We stimulate the same brain regions when we visualize an action and when we actually perform that same action.

Imagine then that you see yourself getting up early, jumping out of bed, excited about getting on with your day. The sun is shining, and you take those first steps out of your bedroom. Now work through where you're going and what kind of activity/career follows on from that feeling of anticipation. By looking at who you are and what you were meant to be doing will create your WOW factor. Rest assured this doesn't happen overnight. It's a process. Just like behavior change, it takes practice, trying and experiencing things that get you closer to your WOW.

*... And WOW is it ever worth it!*

Amy Goldberg

## To Be Your Truth:

Getting closer to your truth means that you're getting closer to identifying what jives you.

Ask yourself the following 3 questions:

1. What subject could I read 500 books about without getting bored?

2. What could I do for five years straight without getting paid?

3. What would I spend my time doing if I had complete financial independence to do anything?

# When Motivation Does Not Work

*We're all going to have crappy days*

What happens when you're feeling so unmotivated that no amount of logic, positive thinking or external support can quell the pain? You either have to succumb or find a way to get past it. There's nothing in between--or is there?

As an inspirational speaker and life & business strategist, I recognize that I need to meet people where they are. Why? -- because no amount of insight or wisdom that I can impart will benefit you when you're not interested in hearing it. You're not hearing it because you're not in the right mindset to receive what I'm saying.

Motivation can be depleted in a number of ways. The feeling of rejection can change your behavior. When you get rejected, you lose your desire to try because it seems as though nobody would care either way. Typically, this isn't the case, and, ye,t when you're rejected by one person, it feels as if you've been rejected by everyone, or, at least, that's what it feels like.

Rejection also tends to obliterate self-control. You'll overindulge, self-sabotage, and soothe your rejected soul. That could mean shopping, overeating, saying yes to things you know aren't good for you. Another way of depleting your motivation is having too much on your mind, too many decisions to make. Remember, you make 35,000 decisions a day--A Day!!! That's crazy. No wonder you're exhausted. Decision fatigue can lead eventually to looking for shortcuts as well as being short on patience with friends, family members, and colleagues. Your brain is tired. All it wants to do is rest. If you don't start to manage the number of choices that you make in a day, you'll find yourself repeating (over and over again) poor habits of overindulging.

**So, what can you do?** Shift your mindset. Take action. In the case of rejection, find ways either to face it head on or walk away. It could be something you may be doing that's caused the rejection, and, therefore, you need to discuss it to find out why. At other times it has nothing to do with you, and, therefore, you must remove yourself from the situation.

When unmotivated, you tend not to take care of yourself. First, pinpoint the problem. What's going on? Are you stuck? Why? Once you've determined why, take one step toward action. Do something that gets you from deciding to doing. Make it a priority. You'll start to see a shift in your mindset by taking action. No, it's not easy. Do it anyway.

Be Your Truth

When you need to get your brain in check, start to list the decisions you foresee you need to make in a given day. Let the rest go. Sure, they'll be unknown decisions that you'll need to make on the fly, and, yet, plan for the main ones. This way you won't feel overwhelmed. Manage what you can. In many cases, there are decisions that you 'feel' you want to make, and, yet, they could easily be made by others. Try and leave your ego out of it.

Last, when you're feeling that you just can't seem to pick yourself up and you have no motivation to do anything …. do ONE THING, anyway. Figure out that 'one thing' that you like (used to like) doing. And **do it**. Move into action. It's the only way you'll break the habit of feeling demotivated. Try. Just try. Soon you'll see that you'll be trying a lot more.

***Trying = Action.*** You've got this!

## To Be Your Truth:

When you can't rely on motivation and inspiration to guide you, get closer to your truth and dig in. Do it anyway. Do that one thing. I'll always encourage you just to start.

Amy Goldberg

## Blah, Blah, Rah, Rah

Do you ever feel as if you're going around in circles? I was at a bookstore the other day, and as I picked up a book and started browsing through it, I started to laugh because I remembered that I had already read it. It seemed really funny to me. I wondered how many other people have picked up books that they've already read. And then it dawned on me. How many personal development books, podcasts, workshops, retreats, speakers does it take for someone to start taking *action* and start moving the needle for himself or herself?

This question is of particular interest to me as I make my living helping others become their full potential, become their truth. I'm my clients' external eyes and ears providing a more accurate picture of their reality, and, yet, I'm not their crutch. I'm more of a good swift kick in their butt. Fortunately, they appreciate it (most of the time).

After three decades of helping others, here's what I've learned. When it gets right down to it, it's a fear of and/or lack of confidence in knowing oneself. More often than not, it's the not knowing how to move ahead with that "thing" that's called one's "calling." That thing that is SHOUTING out at all of us from the depths of our very soul to

## Be Your Truth

say, *PLEASE, I'm begging you to start listening to me. I know what you want. Trust me.*

Since I can remember, my mantra has been (and I'm sure you're sick of hearing this, which is a good thing as it must mean it's starting to stick with you) *It starts with you.* The reason we get discouraged is because we tend to look in every single direction except to ourselves to find the answers. Why? -- because it can get REALLY uncomfortable. We can actually go through our entire lives not understanding the single most important and closest person to us .... and that's OURSELF. And that would be a tragedy. I love seeing when things unfold, and people find their sweet spot. It can take years; it can take seconds; it depends upon how in tune one is with oneself.

For me it took a while. I was always chasing the shining objects flying in my direction. It was exhausting, discouraging, depressing, and caused me great anxiety. I needed to STOP dead in my tracks and say, *ENOUGH.* Once I did, I started moving in a direction that made sense to me toward that "thing" that was tugging at me to take notice. Step by step I started to reverse engineer where I wanted to grow. At the end of the day, and there will be an end, we owe it to ourselves to connect with who we are and what we gravitate toward. Take yourself off auto-mode and start taking action--even if it's small steps. Eventually, the steps will get bigger. Once you build your confidence through action, then the training wheels will come off, and you'll be riding on your own. I'm here to continue to say that *You've got this.*

Amy Goldberg

## To Be Your Truth:

Repeat, repeat, repeat. I'm going to say this as many times as it takes for you to start taking action toward your truth. Your truth is what will pull everything together for yourself. Just try. Don't think. Just do. And that's the truth!

## **Just My Luck**

*You're a lot luckier than you think*

I read an article a while ago: *How To Make Your Own Luck,* by Daniel H. Pink. In the article he highlights the work of Richard Wiseman, head of the psychology research department at the University of Hertfordshire in England. There Wiseman and his colleagues have conducted studies for more than a decade on what makes some people lucky and others not. *What luck! Pretty fascinating stuff, right?*

Wiseman's research showed that luck was not due to *kismet, karma, or coincidence.* Instead, he says, ... *lucky folks, without even knowing it, think and behave in ways that create good fortune in their lives.* The writer goes on to say that *Wiseman found that lucky people are particularly open to possibility. For example, Why do some people always seem to find fortune? It's not dumb luck. Unlike everyone else, they see it. Most people are just not open to what's around them. That's the key to it.* He has a theory and he's sticking to it.

Research has shown that there's a correlation between feeling lucky and being lucky. Lucky people generate their own good fortune. They are attuned to creating and noticing opportunities; they listen to their intuition; they have positive expectations; and they have a resilient attitude that transforms bad luck into good.

In a nutshell, your thoughts create the luck in your life. If you think you're going to be a lucky person, then chances are you're going to experience lots of good fortune. If you think you're an unlucky person, then you're probably going to experience ill fortune. Luck isn't something that happens to you. It's something that you create.

Lucky people are prepared to work hard, to create their good luck. On the flip side, unlucky people are trusting destiny and fate. They believe that it's something that happens to them and, therefore, why bother putting in any effort? When it comes to creating your own luck, a big part of it is how you see yourself and the world. Lucky people attract others. They are positive. They see opportunities, and they make the most of them. When bad things happen, they are resilient; they bounce back. Unlucky people are fatalistic. They are convinced that they are going to experience bad luck, and, hence, if they believe that to be true, they won't put in the effort, and, therefore, it becomes a self-fulfilling prophecy.

According to Richard Wiseman, there are four principles that can create good fortune in both your life and career:

**1. Maximize Chance Opportunities**

Lucky people are skilled at creating, noticing, and acting upon chance opportunities. They do this in various ways which include building and maintaining a strong network, adopting a relaxed attitude to life, and being open to new experiences.

## 2. Listen To Your Lucky Hunches

Lucky people make effective decisions by listening to their intuition and gut feelings. They also take steps to actively boost their intuitive abilities — for example, by meditating and clearing their mind of other thoughts.

## 3. Expect Good Fortune

Lucky people are certain that the future will be bright. Over time, that expectation becomes a self-fulfilling prophecy because it helps lucky people persist in the face of failure and positively shapes their interactions with other people.

## 4. Turn Bad Luck Into Good

Lucky people employ various psychological techniques to cope with, and even thrive upon, the ill fortune that comes their way. For example, they spontaneously imagine how things could have been worse; they don't dwell on the ill fortune, and they take control of the situation.

This reminds me of the book *The Power of Positive Thinking* by Norman Vincent Peale.

You might just say, *I made Luck do it* rather than *Luck made me do it!*

## To Be Your Truth:

Shift your attitude. Approach your truth in a way that creates the space for positivity. It's in you to receive.

# Stop Selling …
# Tag 2 friends If You Like This

What could be holding you back from your truth? Is it that you've got it all wrong? Do you think the by-product of your efforts is the answer? Are you leading with your truth? If you come from a place of ego, then you're not. I get it. It's a dog-eat-dog, an eat-or-be eaten, world. By the way, what's our fixation on being eaten? Oh, it's our survival skills kicking in.

When you take the approach that pushes another person out of the way in order to get to something that you want, you're not leading with your truth unless, of course, your truth is that you're an asshole. And that could be quite possible. However, I'm here to say that you're not really an asshole. There's a whole other thing going on if you're acting like one. That's when you need to dig even deeper.

Having said that, this grabbed me as being really funny. I've been reading on Instagram, Twitter, and Facebook where someone posts what is supposed to be an authentic, sincere message that, in fact, turns out to be completely inauthentic and insincere when at the end of the post, it says, *If you like this, tag 2 friends, or share this, or.....* however, you word it, it's a sales pitch.

On a fairly consistent basis, I read and/or come across the same inspirational messages, thoughtful considerations, heartfelt sentiments, as well as strong messaging to be oneself, etc. For example, I read a post recently that said, *Give fully without the expectation that it will benefit you.* And then it said, I kid you not, *Tag 2 of the most giving friends you know to acknowledge them below.* What? *Me thinks there is a wolf in sheep's clothing.* Apart from sounding glib, Come On!!! You do realize that you're coming off sounding so insincere. We KNOW you're trying to expand your reach, get more *likes, loves, followers,* or whatever it is that you're trying to obtain--by the way--for "yourself."

Why do we turn our messages back to ourselves? If we were truly being sincere, then wouldn't we simply leave the message as is-- with a focus on the intended and then let things unfold as they will? Nope, we don't because we're bombarded with the idea that we constantly need to sell, sell, sell. If we're not selling, then we're promoting. I get it. There's a fine line between the two. Actually, it's not a fine line – it's a **BIG fat** line. We choose (every time) how we want to come across. I don't doubt for a minute that we don't know what we're doing. It's the subtle (not so subtle, really) art of selling ourselves. And yet, it gets old.

Take, for example, some (not all) of those HUGE motivational conventions in which they bring on big name speakers. Behind the scenes, the first thing they ask the speaker before he or she signs is: *What are you going to sell?* Not: *What are you sharing? What are you GOING to sell?* That's how they make money. It's like herding sheep at these things. People get sucked right into the vortex, unaware that it's one big sell-fest. This, however, is not to be confused by other events that are meaningful and have the best of intention and desire to want to help guide and offer support to others.

When you send out messages with the desire truly showing you want to convey, share, impart information to others without asking for anything in return, watch what happens. Try it. People will have a greater appreciation and trust in your message. IF they want to share or tag or do whatever via their own motivation, great! If not, so what? Let it be. Let it go. Deliver your messages for the right intention. If, however, you want to force the message by asking people to *like, follow, whatever,* then be upfront and announce your intention. *I don't care about you; it's all about me.* If you're now thinking, *Well that just sounds insincere.* Guess what? You just answered your own question.

**It's time to get real.**

## To Be Your Truth:

When you know your truth, you will start to lead with your truth. Trust me, it's far more rewarding.

Amy Goldberg

# Emotionally, Speaking

You may have noticed that there's quite a bit of new information emerging about emotional intelligence quotient (EQ). There's a reason for this. With today's emerging technology and fast-growing exploration into robotics, research has shown that a person's EQ will become one's greatest asset, and, in turn, command the attention of potential employers.

*So, what is Emotional Intelligence?*

Emotional Intelligence is how well you identify and manage your own emotions and react to the emotions of others. It's understanding how those emotions shape your thoughts and actions so that you can have greater control over your behavior. In turn, it's having the ability to develop the skills to manage yourself more effectively. You're not curbing your emotions. You're learning to understanding them better.

Emotional Intelligence involves four major skills: *the ability to perceive emotions; the ability to reason with emotions; the ability to understand emotions; and the ability to manage emotions.*

*Why that's important is because ...*

Becoming more emotionally conscious allows you to grow and gain a deeper understanding of who you are, and, in turn, enables you to communicate better with others and build stronger relationships.

*What about at work?*

Imagine you find yourself getting frustrated and angry with a colleague. As you assess your feelings, analyze what you're really upset about .... ask yourself, *Am I really upset about my colleague's actions, or does my anger stem from an underlying frustration and pressure from something other than my colleague?* Perhaps you've just been given more work than you can handle.

Emotionally intelligent people are able to look at the situation and correctly identify the true source of their feelings. It's not always easy. As a matter of fact, it's incredibly difficult for a lot of us. Interestingly, many experts now believe that a person's EQ may be more important than their IQ. It's certainly a better predictor of success, quality of relationships, and overall happiness.

From a success standpoint, higher emotional intelligence helps you become a stronger internal motivator. This motivator can reduce procrastination; it can increase self-confidence and improve your ability to focus on a goal. It also allows you to create better networks of support, overcome setbacks, and persevere with a more resilient outlook. Every emotion has a function. It helps you to gain alignment. Emotions play an important role in helping to direct your behavior.

The most significant emotions are your basic emotions: surprise, disgust, fear, happiness, sadness, and anger. These basic emotions are a part of the natural development of every one of us. They are the same for everyone. They are also associated with an emotional state called a *feeling*. Each of us responds and reacts differently to the emotions that are experienced (a feeling) and, yet, we all have them.

The great news is that emotional intelligence can be learned. It's not something inbred. As we all know, it's never too late to learn anything. By having a better understanding of what EQ is and what you need to know, it can prove to have a positive effect on the rest of your life.

***Now that's something to wrap your head around.***

## To Be Your Truth:

Part of being your truth and living your truth is to understand better your emotions. Why do you respond in a certain way? What triggers your emotions? It's never too late to learn anything. And you can!

## Are You A Person Of Your Word?

I'd like you really to consider if, in fact, you are a person of your word. I say this because, as of late, I've been observing more and more that conversations ending with *Consider it done. Yes, absolutely, I'll send it to you. You can count on me. I will be there. I'll call you then.* (I could go on …) don't necessarily translate into action. In other words, there's no intended, committed action toward what was being said. *Why?* Here's my theory. We seem to have a really hard time saying no. I'll bet that you actually knew before you said it that you weren't really planning on delivering on what you said yes to in the first place.

Here's the irony of that. We say *yes* when we really mean *no* so as not to disappoint another. What happens is the opposite. You're actually making yourself look worse and, in turn, disappointing another. You may never recognize this because the other person may never call you out on your word. You're then left thinking, *Great, no response from the other person. I'm home free.* This fascinates me. It always has. This isn't new and, yet, I've noticed this, as I mentioned, to be more prevalent.

I need to know. Is this your truth? It can't be because it's a lie. It takes a lot more energy to tell an untruth then it does to be straight up. You're exhausting yourself--unnecessarily. The compulsion to say 'yes' when you really mean 'no' does you a real disservice for a number of reasons; For one, you're not building trust. You lose credibility. No one will believe anything that you say if you don't deliver on your actions unless, of course, you let him or her know ahead of time that you're not able to deliver. If nothing is said, then the next time you speak, it's just 'noise' to everybody.

Another reason not to say 'yes' when you're planning on not delivering is that the person you say yes to believes you. He or she isn't having any notions. They're hoping that yes means yes. It also means that you could really be holding things up for that person. They're counting on you.

What's funny is that you're not wanting to disappoint another, or perhaps wanting to show that you're the 'man or woman' of the day, the savior, the one with connections, etc., which is ultimately based on ego, backfires miserably. Ultimately, you come from a place of either wanting to be helpful, as you'd like others to help you when in need, or it's a fear that you don't want to be rejected or abandoned if you say no to someone.

Brené Brown, a research professor in social work, has spent two decades studying shame, empathy and vulnerability. Brown says *"we often don't set boundaries; we let people do things that are not okay and then we're resentful. We tend to imagine that setting a boundary means being rude or pushy. But setting boundaries doesn't mean you're being cold-hearted.* Brown goes on to explain that *One of the most shocking findings of my work was the idea that the most compassionate people I had interviewed over the last 13 years set the most boundaries.*

At the end of the day it really comes down to owning your *'no,'* to have both the confidence and understanding that you're not always going to please everyone-- because you won't. Rather than compromise your good word in order to appease another, tell it as it is. Set your word to action (or not). And, yet, know that when you say you're going to do something ... someone believes you. Someone. Really. Believes. You.

Try it out today. Think before you speak. Speak once you have an answer that you can live by. If things change, well then speak your truth. It really is that simple.

## To Be Your Truth:

First better understand why you feel you need to say *"yes"* when you really mean *"no."* From there, decide if this is who you really want to be. Is this your truth? Start to practice being your truth. It may be uncomfortable at first. Setting boundaries does get easier over time.

Amy Goldberg

## **You're Not Getting It**

You are single-handedly squashing creativity, trust, and your opportunity for real growth in one fell swoop if, in the workplace, you tolerate poor behavior and a lack of care in the ideas people share. Yep, I said it. To quote Howard Beale from the movie NETWORK *I'm as mad as hell, and I'm not going to take this anymore."*

Do I have your attention? So, what's the big deal .... really?

Every single time you curb someone's enthusiasm, squash an idea because you don't like it, you diminish someone's interest in wanting to contribute going forward. Every time you're not paying attention to what someone else is saying or show a lack of interest and common decency toward another, you stifle, muffle, and basically HALT in its tracks any further creative flow. Period. Why? -- because no one will bother to share anything unless he or she HAS to. And, this is not you 'being' your truth.

I have seen firsthand and have received feedback from employees every time I consult at a workplace. It doesn't need to be this way. You can't be expected to grow and develop people, and a company in this manner. It doesn't work. We tend to talk over one another; we are discourteous, and, most important, we tend not to listen. Why? Please tell me. I really want to know.

In today's world where anxiety, depression, and loneliness are on the rise, it's more important than ever to pause and consider others. I'm with Brené Brown, Richard Branson, Simon Sinek, and others who want to create a space for people to have a greater voice, to trust that they will be heard and not discounted.

Too often we play into the bully mentality because it seems so much easier than to experience the wrath of whatever negative consequences bring. I've heard time and time again that people who feel stifled would rather keep quiet than agitate the bullies fearing that things may get worse. And they typically do if there's no resolution.

It takes a change in culture (no easy task) and rethinking to move people and a company's growth forward. And, yet, the results are remarkable. Gone should be the days when we put a blind eye to the bullies because they may be your top salespeople. That's ridiculous. Imagine how many top talent you'd have if those people muddying the waters were no longer there. Change happens when we take action toward the goal of creating a healthier, more positive, and productive environment with a lot more listening going on. It's time.

Amy Goldberg

## To Be Your Truth:

Your truth is to have a voice. Your truth is to be in a working/living environment that speaks to that truth. Bullies need not apply. Using your voice is your truth.

# How Do You Cut Through The Bullsh*t?

How do you cut through all of the bullshit in order to lead your best life? The reality is a lot of us struggle. We look around and think that most people are leading better lives than we are.

And, here lies the number one biggest barrier that has us all screwed up. If you lived your life never having to compare yourself to another person, I bet, for the most part, you would think you were doing pretty well because you would be measuring your life only through your eyes.

When we start to get sucked into having to keep up with others, or we "see" that others are leading these celebrity-like lives, we feel bad about ourselves. We feel that we should be leading the same kind of life. Look at how social media has created an environment where we feel lonelier and more isolated, a life that has us pining for something that we may not even want and, yet, looks so enticing. We have the ability to create any kind of life for ourselves and, yet, we don't believe that we can. We have a lot of limiting beliefs that sabotage any effort toward moving into action-- by that I mean moving into action in a direction that we want to be taking. We may not even know where we want to be going because we're so busy looking around at others.

When you know your truth; the real essence of who you are and what resonates with you in your life; what's important to you; what feeds your heart and soul; what you really need, rather than want, that's when you will start to feel more comfortable in your own being.

Disclaimer. It's not easy. Life gets complicated. There's a lot going on. However, you don't need to make it more complicated. Cutting through the bullshit in your life is about letting go of everything that doesn't serve you. This includes people that bring you down, relationships that aren't healthy and fulfilling, work that doesn't spark you, unhealthy habits that are making you sick, barricading yourself and feeling isolated. Stop this madness. You can pivot. You have the ability to pivot.

Make a move. Take the time to discover what it is that you need in order to be more fulfilled. Don't do it alone. Work with, talk with someone or a group of people that can help guide the discussion to help you get past yourself. You may not know what that is for you just yet. The goal for you is just to start. Take action.

## To Be Your Truth:

We create our own bullshit more often than not. We compare ourselves to others – big mistake. We're so busy looking around that we don't give ourselves credit. Zoom in. Look within. That's the only way you'll find your answers. Let down your guard. Start working on you.

## Overdeliver is Something We Say, Yet Rarely Deliver

You've heard the term: *Talk is cheap and full of broken promises.* There are many sayings that are similar, and, yet, it's too bad we have to use any of them. They all relate to actions that weren't-- well--actioned. I don't believe it's deliberate. I do believe that we come up with creative marketing spins that create the illusion that we're 'all that.' And then we find it difficult to translate that into anything but mediocrity.

It's a shame, especially, since every time I hope for that 'special something' rarely does it appear. If it did though, wow! That 'thing' or business would probably be super successful. Imagine if we all upped our game, provided exceptional service and showed we were all exceptionally kind human beings who had left our homes each morning with open eyes and heart and would go where our curiosity and soul would guide us. Maybe we're all just too tired. Maybe we just can't be bothered to take the extra effort because it's hard enough just putting one step in front of another.

There are many books on the subject of 'over delivering and being exceptional,' etc. And yet we still can't get it right. The saddest part of all of this is when I see store openings. I think about how excited the owners must have been to open a new place. They took their time looking for that perfect spot, one they could afford. Did their market research, etc.? And, then, for what-- to have it shut down within a year? That must be crushing. So, why is that?

Why are we settling? Is it due to lack of interest? It must be so frustrating hiring staff if they approach their work in a lackluster manner. I've even seen owners lack the enthusiasm to wow their customers/clients. Again, I ask, *Why even bother?* In these cases, I believe that the ego has completely taken over.

I met a guy in Los Angeles through a friend of mine. The two of them were best buds since high school. He kept saying, *You have to meet this guy. He's so great.* I did. When we met, we talked about everything. We connected immediately. He said, *We are locked in, friends for life.* He kept saying that over the course of many days and months. You know--*fast friends.* I thought instinctively, *Why does he keep saying friends for life when we just met? What was the need to have to say that? Could it not just evolve?* Why was I thinking this? I think it's because everything he said--everything-- never came to fruition. It was bizarre. And then he vanished.

I bring this up to demonstrate the point that he most certainly wasn't comfortable being in his own soul. He was all over the place. I could feel he wanted to run away from himself. Any distraction suited him perfectly. I also recognized that I was not trusting my truth. I could feel he was insincere. His lips were moving but he wasn't saying anything. I'm positive he had no idea of how he was *being*. And I asked myself – *What was going on with me*--apart from being incredibly disappointed, feeling gypped? My ego was definitely at play. I was hurt. I felt rejected. At this point, being my truth was nowhere to be found. Ah, yes, it was my ego taking over. I sat with this feeling for a while--a long while.

Time passed. Later, I spoke with a few friends and told them what occurred. They shrugged their shoulders to say it's happened to them. This seemed to be commonplace. *What?*

Does anyone see this as being strange? Are we just accepting this to be the norm? I surely hope not. What's going on? Why don't we care? Have we become so slack in our behavior, or, and I suspect this to be true, are we forgetting who we are as human beings?

Are we recognizing that as life becomes more convenient, we've taken it upon ourselves to act that way as well? Are we now a society of convenient behavior, convenient friends, convenient relationships? Have we stopped trying? Yes, I have a lot of questions.

It's time to re-evaluate. Now is the time to reconnect with ourselves and our truth. There's no way you want to live in a world where you can't trust anything anyone says or settle for the lack of quality service.

## To Be Your Truth:

You need to pause. Sit where you are in your life right now. Are you <u>your</u> friend or your foe? Start there. If you don't like yourself, then that's a problem. Then we won't like you either. This then translates into everything that you do.

## Walk To The Right?

Observations in life are the keys to leading with your truth. My observations have led me to call out the absurd in order to have you get closer to your truth. That's probably why I called this section: **Is It Just Me?** Reality is that you sometimes need to get to the stuff that's holding you back before you can smell the flowers. So, here goes ...

We talk a good game. What about living without having to play those games? Here is a case in point. We don't seem to care. We're all blindly bumping into one another. I know it's not just me, and, yet, I feel so isolated in my understanding of human behavior. It's as if people woke up and set out in their "bubble," as if kindness, manners and being courteous became too much of a struggle. It's as if one day people decided to say, *Fuck it. It's ALL about ME, and I don't care anymore. Everyone for himself or herself."*

What am I going on about? In a nutshell, it's this. *Walk to the FUCKING right when you're walking.* I can walk as far to the right where there is no space between me and the wall, and people will STILL bump into me. WTF? What is it about people not being respectful? They see people coming. And it's getting worse.

# Amy Goldberg

I used to run with a friend of mine. We'd run side by side, and then I would sprint in front to form a single line when people were coming our way. I would automatically assume that this was the signal for my friend to get into single line so as to not bump into the oncoming person. Nope. She would hold her ground, and when she did 'slam' into someone, she was shocked – yes--shocked when they yelled at her.

One day I said to her, *You know that I'm not sprinting in front of you to form a single line for training purposes. I'm moving out of the way so that a person has room to walk by. I thought that would be your signal to also move. Why do you hold your ground and bump (bash) into people?* I kid you not. She had a deer-in-the headlights look on her face, as if she had no clue. She said that she hadn't realized. Why-- because she was in her own little world. I said to her, *From now on, we either run in isolated places or we move into single file.* When she remembered, she moved. When she didn't …. She pissed off a lot of people-- including me.

I was walking with husband, Tommy, one Sunday near a university. Students were walking to an event holding signs about compassion and love. There were about 10 of them walking toward us. Tommy and I moved into single file, and STILL they didn't budge. They forced us off the sidewalk. I stopped and said, *Please share the sidewalk.* One of the "compassionate" males actually said, *"No"* (while holding a sign that said *love*). Now, normally, I would have stopped and had a conversation with this group and noted the irony of their 'cause' and the shitty behavior they demonstrated. However, I didn't 'hear' the guy say 'no' until Tommy told me, after the fact. He said, *I'm surprised you didn't say anything to them after the guy said No.* You may be wondering why Tommy didn't say anything. Well, he did. I actually heard someone say, *Fuck off.* Ha, and, yet, I didn't hear it.

You see. Anger feeds anger. We're triggered. We all handle things differently. I like to reason with people. And, yet, in hindsight, I loved his response. When someone says *No* to a common courtesy, well then, fuck you, too! At that moment – that seemed to be my truth--right or wrong.

But I digress. I really want to know why people feel that they can own the road, so to speak, without any consideration for others. With people walking shoulder to shoulder, side by side, I feel as if I'm playing "red rover." I actually loved that game when I was a kid. I liked running as fast as I could trying to break the human wall of locked arms and then swinging on them if I couldn't break through. We would inevitably all fall to the ground. It was fun. Hmmmmm, I could really start a new thing: street games-- dodgeball and red rover. Walk at your own risk. After all, that's what it feels like.

I'm not coming with a resolution here. I'm stating a frustrating point that we can't possibly be THAT selfish, THAT self-absorbed, THAT ignorant, and, yet, YES, YES, and YES again, I say WTF! Do you feel at all put out by this? I guess my first question should be: Do you experience this? Or, are you that person not paying attention and bumping into people? It's exhausting. It's rude. It's time to start looking up and 'seeing' other human beings. We don't need to be competing for real estate on the sidewalk. There IS enough space for all of us.

So, why does this irk me so much? Apart from lack of consideration, it condones what I've been saying all along. The more inconsiderate we are, the further away we get to our truth. There's no way we all want to be assholes. That's not who you are.

## To Be Your Truth:

Start looking up. Become more aware of your environment. If you lead your life with a me-centric approach, you're going to be awfully lonely. To be your truth is to be kind. Practice looking around. You'll notice a lot more.

## Keep Telling Yourself That

I was introduced to a book called *"Overdeliver"* by Brian Kurtz, a marketing book and, yet, it's so much more than that. I'm convinced that until we become more self-aware, none of these books will truly make a dent. It boggles my mind how many examples I can cite where one is either in the wrong 'service' business or that one went into the business knowing that he or she struggled in this area and had no desire to improve.

There's a great store that sells clothing with fabulous uplifting messages on them. There are similar items that make you feel that 'love is all around.' There's even a sweatshirt in the window on a mannequin that says *Love More*. I think the store name is even warm and fuzzy. The owner, however, and I see her at least a few times a week as I walk by, is anything but 'warm and fuzzy' unless she's selling something. And, even then, she's not so happy.

Here's the thing. I'd LOVE to buy something from her again, but I won't enter the store anymore. Her energy brings me down. I see that others feel the same way as they walk in and out without as much as a "hello" or "welcome" from the owner. Hey, I don't know what's going on in her life. What I do know is that there is an inauthentic vibe that does not reflect what she's selling. And that means, that's not what she's all about.

Similarly, when hiring staff, an owner should make sure, at the very least, that the person/ people care about what it is that they're doing. Another example is that educational organizations that teach those trying to transition into other careers or wanting to learn new skills should be taught how to communicate effectively. Businesses have reached out to me, asking if I'd be interested in speaking at their evening event where they wanted to celebrate their staff, volunteers, and alumni. One wanted a professional high energy motivational speaker. The Executive Director did mention to me that they've been looking for months to find the right person. We had a call. The Communications Director was also on the call. Great call-- or so I thought.

They felt pleased that I'd be the one to deliver their message. They asked if I'd capture our conversation and send them the highlights of what we discussed along with my fee. I did so within an hour of our call. They mentioned to me that they had less than an attractive budget, so I discounted my fee by more than 60% and sent the Message.

Crickets. Not a peep. Weeks went by. The date was only a month away. My calendar was filling up. I don't hold dates unless confirmed. So, what did I do? I called her. A woman on the other end answered. She sounded very familiar. It was the Communications Director that I had spoken with on the phone. I didn't announce myself. I simply said, *Hello! May I please speak to ……. One moment. Pause, pause, pause ….* She then said *What's your name?* I told her who I was …. Ha, the call went right to voice message. I, of course, left a message.

Look, I didn't need to call her. I suspect that my fee may have been cost prohibitive. But, come on ... they reached out to me! I took my time to speak with them, put together a synopsis of our call. Clearly, they were excited BEFORE I sent my fee. You're an EDUCATIONAL ORGANIZATION teaching people how best to handle themselves, teaching life skills ... and you don't have the grace or courtesy to call back and have the conversation around whatever the reason was why had you NOT called back--especially when they wanted to convey a motivational, inspirational message at their event? By the way, they eventually did call me back. They apologized. They decided not to have a speaker as it was cost-prohibitive.

A friend of mine works at a therapy center. The center has practitioners in physiotherapy, massage, athletic therapy, etc. My friend is one of the best massage therapists around, an amazing therapist. She loves her clients and cares deeply about their health and wellbeing. She's even in her third year studying Chinese medicine, a tough course.

I asked her how she was enjoying her new work because she recently moved from one clinic to this one. She said *I love my clients, but the company is into hard sales. They meet with all the practitioners once a week to make sure we are all referring so that clients see more than one therapist.* She went on to say, *There's a lot of pressure to sell.* She's not comfortable doing that.

Once again, company XYZ, this is not an inauthentic approach to sell for the sake of selling. Reason number 1: You're asking the therapists to refer for the sake of referring. 2: You really don't care about your client's well-being. It's a cash grab. Word gets around. Once people know that you're all about the bottom line – say bye bye.

There are so many examples of this that I could dedicate an entire book to this one topic.

What's it going to take for you to Be your truth, Speak your truth, and Act your truth? Imagine if for one day you became acutely aware of your behavior, your actions, and your mindset. What would you learn about yourself? We have a false sense of ourselves, a false idea as to how we are in this world, how we act toward one another.

Keep telling yourself that you're kind, compassionate, loving, and fabulous, and then go BE that because I truly believe behind the armor that we all carry, we CAN be that. We can live that.

## To Be Your Truth:

Take a really hard look at your actions and see if they are aligned with what you believe and who you are. Start to observe how you are in the world. Ask yourself, *How do I act? Is it consistent with how I show up in the world?*

## Neutral Face

Have you ever watched an episode of *Comedians in Cars Getting Coffee* with host Jerry Seinfeld in which he had Tina Fey as a guest? She was talking about a friend of hers who, when in 'neutral' mode, had a less than flattering face. This is the face we show when we're walking and/or doing anything that doesn't require us to talk or engage with others. Apart from its being hilarious, the episode made me notice people's neutral faces. I imagine it's pretty tough to hold a smiley neutral face. So, hence the reason why I see so many frowns or turned down mouths.

They're everywhere. And, in fact, they are not pleasant looking. The expression of your neutral face, I believe, is one of those rare moments when you're being your true self. This neutral expression (which, by the way, is anything but neutral – it's rather contorted) is something that comes right from our soul. It reflects a lot of who we are when we're not paying attention. Sometimes, I can actually feel people thinking.

If you ever get a glimpse of your neutral face in the mirror, I bet it'll change just as soon as you think, *I need to see what my neutral face looks in the mirror.* Guaranteed--because now you're aware of it. We're great actors. I know, however, when I'm feeling the love in my heart, my neutral face is relaxed, warm, and open. When I'm not feeling myself (so to speak), I can look intense.

One day I was walking down the street and thought I saw someone I knew. I texted the person afterwards to say, *I thought I saw you today.* The person texted back saying, *Yes, you did. I didn't stop you as you looked as if you were a person on a mission.* That translates into "intense." After thinking about it, I knew it was true. I was walking fast. I was thinking fast, and I'm sure that my face looked as if I were constipated. Ha, I'm sure of it. This is when I knew that I needed just to slow the hell down and be in the moment. It's tough. We are either thinking about the past or living in the future. Even when we can rationalize that *all we have is now,* we have a heck of a time living it.

All this is to say that we need to pay more attention to what our body is revealing to us. Fact--we are one with our mind, body and soul. It shows up for us and manifests itself in many ways – even in our 'neutral' face. I ask you-- what would a relaxed, open, and kind expression of yourself look like on your face? Try it and see. I should say *Feel it and see.*

## To Be Your Truth:

Visualize how your neutral face would be if you were the expression of an open, relaxed, kind person. What would that look-like for you? Start paying attention to how you are when no one is looking. All kidding aside-- how is your face showing up?

# PART 3
# BE YOUR TRUTH

At this point in our journey together, I'm trusting there's been a moment of truth. The moment where you've discovered that you're more remarkable then you think. Where you understand your truth, so you can now be your truth.

Amy Goldberg

# BE Your Potential

*You're not stuck*

If you've ever come from a motivational workshop, experienced a Tony Robbins-esque coaching session or intense personal development course, you may have felt as if you were coming down from a super sugar high or, worse, you may have felt downright depressed. Why is that? Could it be that you're searching for what could be rather than how to be?

Zig Ziglar, author and motivational speaker, was famous for his Be, Do, Have philosophy. Its premise was that you have to "Be" the right kind of person first; then you must "Do" the right things before you can expect to "Have" the things in life that really matter. OK, but how? Before you start to search outside yourself, you first need to ask, *Where does my energy come from? What does MY voice say?* You noticed I didn't say *What does my voice tell me?* because we tend to tell ourselves lies. We are misinformed by what we hear rather than what we know to be true for us. Only when you find your authentic self, that true voice, have you found YOUR voice. The essence of your energy IS who you need to BE.

Be Your Truth

We tend to ignore our voice and what resonates with us because it may not be conventional. If you allow yourself to create the space needed for you to BE your voice, then watch what happens. It starts with suspending disbelief, trusting your instincts, letting go and staying curious. Better yet, live your 6-year-old self. What? Yes. That's where your true authenticity and your "anything's possible" mindset will flourish.

Another key to finding your voice, your vibe is consistency. If you're not consistent in trying to create the space needed to become your best version of you, then you'll remain stuck. If you're tired of your way of being, for whatever reason, and it doesn't serve you, then go back to the beginning and ask yourself again, *Where does my energy come from?* In turn, you will begin to identify your true BEing.

For more years than I care to remember, I have discovered through my own work that once one understands and connects with his or her being, one becomes his or her BE. And that's not a grammatical error. *Your voice is your energy. Your vibe is your being. BE THAT.* – Amy G

***How are you BEing?***

## To Be Your Truth:

It's not easy for a lot of people just to 'be.' It can get uncomfortable. Take notice and see how you 'sit' with yourself. Can you just be in the moment? Can you be in your space and contemplate where you are? What does that feel like for you?

# Inspiring From Within

*Uh, oh, it's back to 'you' again*

What happens when an inspirational speaker and coach finds himself or herself not so inspired or motivated? I see and listen to a lot of personal development speakers to hear what they have to say. It's research for my own work. It's interesting to me to watch and listen to people both on and off the stage. I need to know if they're going through the motions or if they really believe what they're conveying. I always hope and trust it's the latter.

Of course, motivational and inspirational speakers and coaches are going to have days, weeks, maybe months when they don't feel so motivated and inspired themselves. Think about it. Psychiatrists see psychiatrists to help put some perspective around things, to help them cope. Personal trainers hire personal trainers to help motivate and keep them in great shape. Why would this be any different? We all experience each day differently from the day before. Some days we leap out of bed; other days it's a struggle. Some days we feel on top of the world; other days we doubt ourselves.

Our brains are complex and magnificent instruments. They wire, fire, and ignite in ways that still baffle those that study them. We're constantly discovering and exploring ways to better understand how it all works. Despite all of this rational thinking, however, we find ourselves adapting and adjusting to our emotional selves. And then ...*it hit me. I, too, found myself not so inspired and motivated.*

It was as if everything I was sharing with others didn't work for me. Or, perhaps, I was way too close to my emotions to see anything else. Maybe I didn't want to see anything else. It was then that I started questioning everything that I was doing, evolving into, honing into after 30 years of work and experiences. I was questioning my worth. What was THAT all about? I was playing mental chess, saying, *If I do this, then I'll feel that.*

Then I paused, knew that this too shall pass and thought, *Wait a minute. If I didn't feel or have these thoughts, then how could I possibly better be able to understand others when I'm working through their challenges. And then you know what happened ... ?* I started facing my doubts, insecurities, and uncertainties. I needed to put things into perspective for myself. If I was questioning what I was doing, then I needed to see for myself what that was.

I thought *Ok, where do I start? How do I make myself see what I was doing and better understand how I was feeling?* I've been saying to others for as long as I can remember, and by now you know it by heart, "It Starts With You." That was my answer. I started to read all of my talks and publications, reading each piece one by one. A wave of confidence and reassurance flooded over me. I burst into laughter. In reading my own work, I actually became motivated and inspired! And then I thought, *Ha. It was there all along ... right there before my eyes.*

*I know what I'm doing. This is what I love to do. Inspiring and helping others to thrive IS my calling. I am good at this.*

After I breathed a sigh of relief (trust me I was relieved), I recognized that, of course, this doesn't mean that I won't have these pangs of self-doubt, uncertainty, and insecurity again. I know I will. I just need to remind myself that these moments of uncertainty make me stronger. You know--*What doesn't kill you, makes you stronger.* I don't like feeling insecure, and, yet, I do know that it certainly makes me a better coach and strategist for others. We all have moments of self-doubt and insecurity. What we need to do is to step back and begin seeing within ourselves.

And remember .... *We need to start by inspiring from within.*

## To Be Your Truth:

It's important to note that sometimes being uninspired will get you closer to yourself, closer to your truth. It sucks to feel unmotivated and uninspired, and, yet, once you stop to see what's going on, it's then that you can build yourself up.

Amy Goldberg

# Mindset Vacation

*We need to give ourselves a break*

You may have heard this referred to as 'Vacation Mindset.' And, yet, there lies the problem for me. It feels temporary. It also feels that in order to feel better, I need to get away. I'm by no means slamming vacations. I LOVE planning and going on vacation. It's when I feel the need to vacate my life is when I need to regroup and figure out why I'm feeling this way. When, however, I do feel the need to get out of dodge, what I do is ... **Shift my mindset.**

This involves first reflecting on where I am in my life right then. Do I feel that I need a vacation? Am I anticipating after my vacation is over that I'll dread the feeling of coming back to my 'life?' Let's bring this closer to home for you. Do you live for your weekends? If so, why? What is it that's not working in your day-to-day life? What I find is that a lot of busy people don't take the time to stop and look at the life they're in.

Life is complicated. And it can toss you on your head. Maybe you're not that great at anticipating pitfalls and bumps in the road. Who is? And, yet, if you like the direction in which you're going, you can handle the bumps. If not, then you may tend to feel every single bump as if they were mountains.

**Here's what you can do:**

Take yourself off autopilot and consciously start to construct a plan in which you are actively doing things; taking action--small steps to putting yourself in a more positive mindset.

You need to stop looking outside of yourself. You can actually give your brain a vacation while going for a walk or taking yourself out of your routine. These are all choices that you can make to rethink positively and reposition your mindset.

If you find yourself routinely doing things because you've *always done them that way and, yet, it's not working for you anymore,* then it's time to make a change. Try replacing or shifting your attention to something else that will energize you. I'm not suggesting that you don't take vacations. Vacations are a healthy way to shake up your environment, get creative, experience more and seek out adventure. It's when you feel the need to run away is when you need to face yourself head on and find out why you want to flee. This is one way you can tap into what's really going on in your head and in your heart. Then ask yourself, *Are they aligned*? If not, why not? Go deep diving and find the sun that shines within YOU. Now, that's where your *mindset vacation* truly lives.

## To Be Your Truth:

If you're experiencing the need to flee, and you're waiting for something like the weekend or a vacation or anything that isn't in the *'now,'* take a look within and see where you're not feeling happy, motivated, or inspired. Face it--head on.

## No Validation Required

*I'm ok; you're ok*

We're human. We need to connect. We need to feel that we belong, that we're part of a community, tribe, sector, institution, organization, group, team, or other. And, yet, it's more than that. We need to feel validated by those around us. Although we don't always admit it, we do care what others think of us. We want others to think well of us. You know--you want the feeling you feel when you see that little 'Like' thumb on Facebook or 'Heart' on Instagram that SCREAMS validation.

The need for validation started when we were learning to become human. When we did something right, we would be rewarded, validated. In fact, as toddlers, every clap, every smile told us that we were doing something right. We wanted more. So we kept seeking approval. We seek validation because we don't always trust ourselves enough to make our own decisions. Sometimes, however, we can lose sight of ourselves, our own judgement. We need to work on and practice being self-confident, to start trusting our own judgement. Our gut doesn't lie. We feel it before we even think it.

**So, why do we feel we need for validation?**

Feeling validated builds our self-esteem or so we think. OK, let's take this one step further. If validation builds our self-esteem, then negative reinforcement must diminish our confidence. If we put the same emphasis on the negative, it could paralyze us. Eek. Consider this: rather than take the position of needing to feel validated, think of yourself as a contributor. You're contributing your knowledge, skills, experience, passion, enthusiasm, and, most important, yourself to whatever you do. That means something. It means that you know how good you are, that you don't need to feel validated. When you do, sure it's a nice feeling, and, yet, YOU already knew it. Let's work on needing less validation and focusing on our own self-worth.

### An Exercise:

Here are some actions you can take to start reinforcing your self-confidence:

**Become Aware of Your Actions**. Check in with yourself. The next time you doubt yourself, ask why, what's going on, how often do you feel this way.

**Ask Yourself Why You're Seeking Approval**. Comprehending why you're seeking approval is the first step toward better understanding how to eliminate the need for it.

**Develop a Greater Sense of Self-Worth**. Self-worth is knowing you are loved, valuable, and worthy because you are and not for any reason other than that. We tend to seek approval from others when our self-esteem is low.

**Practice Self Love**. Be kind to yourself. Practice self-compassion. Self-care is important to your emotional wellbeing.

**Journal Your Thoughts**. Writing is therapeutic. It helps you to figure out your internal struggles.

**Stop Comparing Yourself to Others**. We are all unique individuals. We all have a unique purpose and life journey. We truly don't know what's going on in the lives of others. Social media tends to create a 'smoke and mirrors' effect. Follow YOUR path.

**Trust Yourself**. Don't let anyone else tell you your choices aren't good enough. Hold onto your truth.

Repeat after me ...*I am who I am. Your approval is not needed.* ~ author unknown

## To Be Your Truth:

Receiving a compliment is one thing; seeking others' approval is something else. Work through the exercises above. They will boost your self-confidence. Remember, you're a contributor in this world. Make sure you're also contributing to yourself.

Amy Goldberg

# Now What?

The *Now What?* is happening right now. *What is it for you? What are you doing? Where are you going?* The answers are within you to reveal. I promise you they're there. If you haven't found your truth, then you're not digging deep enough. And you may not be listening.

There could be something else holding you back. The truth is that it's helpful to identify whether you have a fixed or growth mindset. Professor Carol Dweck wrote a book called *Mindset* which explains and describes where we're starting from, what our mindset is telling us about ourselves. It's very revealing. Not to get too detailed, and in a nutshell, Dweck's research showed that, and I quote: *Your view of yourself can determine everything. If you believe that your qualities are unchangeable — the fixed mindset — you will want to prove yourself correct over and over rather than learn from your mistakes.* Dweck goes onto say that *Changing our beliefs can have a powerful impact. The growth mindset creates a powerful passion for learning. Why waste time proving over and over how great you are when you could be getting better?*

Having said this, it's relevant to note how important the right frame of mind is in your journey to self. Your ability to learn, grow, and experience is unlimited. However, if you hold limiting beliefs, then it's going to limit what you think you're capable of accomplishing.

I bumped into a friend that I hadn't seen in years. I gave her a hug. She started by saying how horrible life had been since last we met. She had to move out of her home due to various work problems. She struggled to pay the rent. She ended up moving to her mother's where her sister also resides. She's now helping to take care of her mother and, yet, the circumstances are not ideal. Both her mother and sister are orally abusive. She said, *they blame me for everything.* How horrible!

As we talked, it seemed that her world was crashing beneath her. As her eyes were welling up with tears, we talked about the first thing she thought she needed to do to help herself. It was to get a steady gig where she could become financially self-sufficient. She said that it was a struggle that although she was great at connecting with people, what happened was that she gave a lot of her work away. When it came time to discuss being paid for her work, she heard crickets. We talked about that. Going forward, I suggested that she not devalue her worth. She was great at what she did. It was time for her not to give in to self-doubt and limiting beliefs but to demonstrate her worth, not by giving her work away, but by demonstrating what she could do. This wasn't easy for her to wrap her head around because she was already struggling emotionally. However, what she was doing wasn't working. We started from the place of *What do you need to do. What's the outcome that you're hoping for?* From there we worked backwards to make a plan that seemed reasonable to her.

You see, half the challenge is actually doing something. If I started spewing all the things that she needed to do and she was simply not going to buy into it, then that wouldn't help anyone. You need to break things down in a way in which you're going to act. Your *'now what'* is every step that you take toward what you need and want in order to get closer to *being your truth*.

## To Be Your Truth:

Stop looking around to find the answers. Your *'now what'* is NOW. If you're going through the motions or finding yourself in a tough situation, you can pivot. Even if you feel confined--Pivot. Make another decision. If you feel paralyzed, that's fear. You must get out of your own way. The fear isn't as real as you think it is. Start trusting yourself.

## Wherever You Go, There You Are

*Do you know where you're going?*

I love this: **Wherever You Go, There You Are.** Jon Kabat-Zinn, creator of the Stress Reduction Clinic and the Center for Mindfulness in Medicine, wrote a book with the same title in which he described that in order for us to get to know who we really are, we need to pause in our experiences long enough actually to feel the present moment.

Let's think about that for a moment. When you read the words: **Wherever. You. Go. There. You. Are.**, does it resonate with you or did you skim over it without gleaning any real sense of connection? What I find interesting is that despite the fact that we try so hard to be happy, we're no further ahead in where we want to be and how we want to feel. We may not even know how to get there. We tend to work toward creating the life we think we should be living. If, however, we truly tapped into ourselves, our inner wisdom and instincts, we'd probably lead very different lives. Why? -- because we spend most of our waking hours wanting to be something or someone else. So, when I say, *Wherever you go, there you are,* I mean it literally. I would say that we spend a great deal of time trying to get away from being with ourselves.

Imagine, however, if the opposite were true. Imagine that you actually liked your own company. You would probably be a happier, more fulfilled, loving, kinder, giving human being. Your relationships would be better. You'd like what you were doing. You'd feel more fulfilled and passionate about your life. You'd have more adventures, more fun, more laughs. You wouldn't feel that you HAD to wait for people to join you if you really wanted to do something. You'd do it anyway.

Imagine if you took the time really to get to know yourself. Perhaps you've already discovered the magic of YOU. Perhaps this image I'm painting is you personified. Fabulous. Please tell us. Teach us. We will follow your example. Oh, but wait. Isn't that where we start to get further away from ourselves? You see what I mean? The first thing that we tend to do when we're lost is to look elsewhere, at someone else's life. Here's the thing – OK, yes, I'm going to say it again-- you must start with YOU. You need to take the time--yes, time (you're worth it) -- to get to know who you are. It's a process. It doesn't happen overnight.

**Here's one way to start:**

*Take yourself out on a date. After the date, ask yourself, will there be a second? Were you fun, engaging, interesting to yourself?* I'm being serious. Try it. Hey, if you're someone who would never go out for a meal on your own, you may actually like it, knowing that you'll be there!

Jon Kabat-Zinn discovered that through meditation we could get closer to understanding ourselves better. I know what you might be thinking: *I was following you right up until this point, and then you had to throw in the whole meditation thing.* Meditation has gotten way too complicated when, in actual fact, it's simply about being yourself and knowing something about who you are. It's about coming to recognize that you are on a path whether you like it or not--namely, the path that is your life. Meditation may help us to see that this path has direction Everything that we do now influences what happens next. Take a look around from time to time to see the path that you're on and the direction you're taking.

It's incredibly freeing knowing that nothing more is required of you than just to be fully present, in the here and now. For some reason, we are horrible at doing that. We have so many expectations of ourselves. And, yet, we don't even know who we really are. And, worse, we could be setting expectations that we may not even want for ourselves. *Life is now. There was never a time when your life was not now, nor will there ever be.* - Eckhart Tolle

Here's what I'd like you to consider. Be in the moment. It means having the courage to know you will never be someone other than who you are. If you're not satisfied being you, then **your first call to action** is to get to know yourself better. Give a shout out to yourself.

*Remember:* Wherever You Go, There You Are. *And that's* GREAT!

Amy Goldberg

## To Be Your Truth:

Get to know yourself better. Your mission is to *Take yourself out on a date.* Hopefully, there will be a second, third, fourth ….

## Your Truth

So, what do I mean by Be Your Truth and not fearing it? Yes, we are all coming from different places in our lives, and, yet, all of us need to connect to our truth if we are truly going to lead happier lives. The irony is that it takes an awakened experience for us to identify who we are and what our truth is. This is why a mid-life crisis is so profound. It's not about wanting to be younger or recapturing our youth. It's about actually, for the first time, exploring what exactly we're all about. We've decided to take ourselves off autopilot and start to deep dive into what it is that we really need and want.

The misconception is that it's actually a desire, a thing outside of us. But it's in us. It's in us to identify and explore. As evolving human beings, it takes us time to sit with ourselves. We're so much in our thoughts and the thoughts of others, and the noise is so deafening that we can't feel our soul. We can't identify what it is that has us feeling uncomfortable.

I do know within my own life; I wasn't fully comfortable settling into my skin. I felt an unease, an unsteadiness to trust myself. It wasn't for a lack of confidence. I had that. And, yet, that confidence was coming from a place of ego. My ego was guiding me. I wasn't allowing or empowering my true self to express itself. Every time I would get closer to my spiritual or soulful self, I felt derailed. This, of course, was my choice. I didn't choose me. I chose what others thought me to be and led with that. I wasn't being true to who I was.

This would always come down to the question of *How do I feel? and What was I thinking?* Growing up in a less coddled generation, I didn't have parents who were at my beck and call all the time. They didn't come to my sporting events or extracurricular activities. Rarely did I get driven to places. I walked or got a ride with my friends. Kids were fairly independent and, yet, I knew I needed more guidance finding the direction I wanted to go in. I couldn't find anyone to help guide the journey mainly because I didn't know what to ask. I didn't know what I was feeling.

As a popular, fun loving kid in school, I sat on the student council and was President of my house. I attended a large high school where each student belonged to a house with about 400 students per house. There was a President for each of the 6 houses. Apart from that, I struggled scholastically.

I struggled to memorize for tests; I sucked at math much to my father's chagrin, although he never said anything. He was brilliant. My father was a professional engineer who helped build the first jet engine with Frank Whittle. He went to M.I.T. and was on the Dean's List 5 times. He tried to help me, but he kept teaching me 'old' math-- same results, longer equations.

My older sister stepped in and saved the day. She helped me to make sense of it all. My best subjects were art, English, gym, drama, and marketing. As I mentioned, I thrived in the creative areas. That was my truth. I was kidding myself if I was going to force a square peg into a round hole.

I have to say that I never let fear get in my way. I learned by doing. I didn't care if I failed. I took those failures as a way to grow. I learned more by failing. And, yet, a lot of us fear failure. I felt I had nothing to lose. I'm hoping you, too, will get past the fear. But, first, you need to identify what your fears are.

How would you answer these? Let's get closer to your truth.

Identify Your Fear:
_____
Identify Your Truth:
_____
Identify What Actions You Can Take Today To Get Closer To Your Truth:
_____

## To Be Your Truth:

Your truth is closer than you think. Push fear aside to get closer to your truth. Identify what's holding you back and then what actions you can take today to move past your fears.

Amy Goldberg

# Moments of Truth

As I contemplate the notion of knowing your truth, I often wonder whether some people believe that living their truth is ego driven. We know that it isn't. The ego is counter opposite to our truth. In fact, our truth is stronger than we know. If you choose, you can rise above your ego if you trust yourself enough to 'be.' You may tend, however, to mask feelings of truth depending upon how you're feeling day to day. You may think that your ego dictates your truth because it's times when you're feeling strong with bursts of confidence or a feeling of empowered self that you think you see your truth.

And, yet, I ask you, what happens when you have moments when you question yourself and hold limiting beliefs? Do you doubt your truth then? When do you begin to embody your truth? The truth that is you, you in any state of being. These are things I think about. I believe that the overriding aspect of what holds you back and/ or stops you from doing what you know to be true is fear. And, in reality, fear is not your enemy. In actual fact, it goes much deeper than that. It's your inability to embrace your intuition, to trust yourself, to trust your truth, and, to make things even harder, to live your trust.

How do like them apples? It's a lot to take it. Imagine, however, if you started to trust yourself. You would eliminate "maybes" to get to "yes" and "no" with greater ease. You would eradicate self-talk to create a frictionless flow-- your new reality. And you would unleash life on your own terms-- you, being unapologetically you. That sounds great to me! I'm not sure you recognize this, but you are the love you've been waiting for. That may sound schmaltzy, and, yet, it's true.

It's kind of exciting that you hold the key. If you've metaphorically *'locked yourself into a cage,'* then use your key to unlock it. Dive into the *"never been seen before"* YOU because you hold the power to be empowered. You had the key all along. The question is: *What are you going to do about it now that you know?*

You can't just go back to the same old, same old now that you know that it starts with you. Or will you? I guess the question is, *What's it going to take for you to start embracing your fears so you can reveal your truth to create the life that you want?* That's a mouthful. It's worth re-reading. Go ahead. Re-read it. I'll wait. It's worth absorbing.

It's not easy going from autopilot to putting yourself into gear. It takes energy and effort. At the end of the day, you may be thinking that you're too exhausted just trying to lead your life to even think about making it better. There lies the problem. You need first to identify that "YOU" are a priority, that you come first above all else. It is not a selfish act. In fact, you are better able to serve others when you have discovered your truth--how to be your truth.

It starts by acknowledging the times when you feel fear. I know, for example, that my fear is grounded in what I learned at a very early age. This doesn't come from my experiences but from those of my father and my mother and from their father and mother, from generations way before my birth when circumstances and conditions were very different. And, yet, we believe what our parents tell us until we, well, don't, until we figure things out for ourselves. It takes a long time to reprogram what we've learned if it hasn't served us well. It's not easy. It is, however, worth it.

As we take this journey together, I'm going to encourage you to take mindful notes of where you are. Start to think about and then identify your fears. Are they real or imagined? If they haven't happened yet, then they're imagined. Once you start to face your fears, invite them in as friends. You will quickly recognize that they have always been there to protect you. You now need to let fear know that it can stand down, that there is nothing to fear. This is your moment of truth, the moment when you decide that fear is a friend not a foe, that you have a choice in what you do and how you will respond.

## To Be Your Truth:

Face your fear. Write down what you're afraid of. Go back to the exercise in which I asked what your fears were. If you haven't overcome some of your fears, the fears that are stopping you in your tracks, then you need to keep going with it. Keep addressing *What's the fear that's holding me back?*

# You Are Your Own Hero

## *Start believing it*

As I mentioned earlier, I love the saying; *Wherever you go. There you are.* It's cute. People seem to get a chuckle out of it. And, yet, I hadn't given much thought to the deeper meaning. Every one of us is unique. We have qualities, personalities, and capabilities unlike anyone else. That's incredible!! **You're incredible!** We spend every second of every day with ourselves. So, having said that, how would you answer the following questions:

1. How do you treat yourself?

2. Are you your own best friend?

3. Are you kind to yourself?

4. Do you honor your mind, heart, and soul?

5. Are you leading a fulfilled life that is worthy of who you are?

And the biggest question I have for you: *Have you given any thought to any of this?*

One thing I hope that you take away from this is knowing that **You Are Your Own Hero**. If you're not, you need to be. We are so busy being told to mirror, follow, shadow people whose lives we want to emulate. They say, *If you want to be successful* ..... blah blah blah ..... follow what they do and how they do it. Read that back to yourself. Does this make any sense to you?

First, who are 'they?' And why do you want to be anyone other than yourself?

We have no idea who people really are-- only what they want us to know and believe Imagine if you took the time really to get to know yourself, to discover who YOU really are. That's the person you want to get to know better. Certainly, you glean knowledge and information that resonates with you from a number of different people and sources, and, yet, ... it's when we become groupies, followers, worshippers that we can lose ourselves.

We start to lose our confidence, our self-esteem, our own instincts and gut-check. We start to doubt ourselves and begin to rely on others to give us the answers.

In *No Validation Required,* which you read earlier, I touched on the importance of loving yourself and not comparing yourself to anyone else. Words such as these don't always manifest into action. We tend to question ourselves. If you find yourself identifying way too much with someone other than yourself, then I ask you please to consider, and ....

# Be Your Truth

*STOP yourself when you start to sound like a mimic or paraphrase someone else (too much).*

*STOP yourself when you start putting someone other than yourself on a pedestal.*

*STOP yourself when you fail to see YOU in the big picture.*

*STOP yourself when your gut is telling you something that doesn't ring true for YOU.*

What I'd like to suggest is for you to:

*START trusting yourself.*
*START knowing what your true capabilities are.*
*START tapping into your unique qualities.*
*START following your dreams--YOUR dreams-- Not someone else's.*
*START taking action!*

**START Following YOU!**

## To Be Your Truth:

Take time to get to know yourself better. Put yourself on a pedestal.

Amy Goldberg

# Wrestling With Yourself

Life is a battlefield. Pat Benatar wrote that. She wasn't wrong. Life can get pretty confusing and messy. We're constantly looking around for someone to help us, someone to believe in us, someone to give us a break. It doesn't matter who you are in this world. If you think you don't need anyone, guess again. We all need someone to buy our products, give us money, hire us, love us, trade with us, support us.

We came into this world needing care. Someone had to feed us, clothe us, help us in some way. No one came into this world alone. Even if abandoned, you still had someone care for you when you were a baby. At the center of all of this is you-- you trying to lead your life within the conditions that you're in--life conditions that are based on many determining factors such as where you were born, the circumstances in which you were born, your environment, your family, or absence of family, the abundance or lack of love you received. The list is long, and, yet, I hope this helps to illustrate the point that some have to wrestle with challenging life conditions that can test the very depth of their soul. Others will have an easier go of it. However, I do know that it is your fortitude that gives you the ability to be resilient and adaptable. This strength and determination give you (even if it's a

Be Your Truth

glimmer within you) a greater chance for creating the life that you want to see for yourself.

Here's where I'm going to ask you to pause. This is where you need to ask yourself the tough question: *Do I believe I'm worthy of being my truth?*

Let's lay it out. Your truth <u>could</u> be:

- You always wanted to be [fill in the blank] but settled for [fill in the blank] instead
- You want to go back to school and learn something new, but you feel you're too old
- Your armor is that you're a tough guy, but, really, you're nothing like that
- You appear to be sweet and shy, but, really, you have so much to say
- You want to be honest with someone you care about but are afraid to have the conversation
- You are angry about people who have hurt you but are afraid to approach them
- You know you're great at something but are too afraid to do it
- You are afraid, and you don't know how to ask for help
- You want to make changes in your life but are too afraid to make changes

- You are an independent person but feel tied down in a relationship that's not working
- You want a greater voice at work but are afraid you'll get fired
- You help others before you help yourself
- You live with constant guilt and want to stop feeling controlled
- You want to live your life your way but don't know how

These are just the tip of the iceberg. If nothing from this list resonates with you, then keep going. It's time to declare your truth. What exactly is your truth? Lay it out. Make a list. Write it down. Don't think about it. Feel it. Just start writing. It's time. Stop wrestling with yourself. Start embracing who you are.

## To Be Your Truth:

What's your truth? Lay it out. Make a list. Write it down. Don't think about it. Feel it. Just start writing.

## Mindset on a T-Shirt

Consider this for a second. You're walking down the street and, typically, if people are walking alone, they usually avoid eye contact or look at you with a *What are you looking at* expression. Or, perhaps they're deep in thought, or on their smartphone. My point is that even when you do look at people straight in the eye and smile and say *Hello,* you are met with a number of different reactions. Sometimes you even get a *"hello"* back.

I often think that it would be funny if that same person whom you said hello to and didn't reply back, was thinking that you're probably a weirdo and was later introduced to you by a mutual friend. THEN that person would, of course, say *hello* and probably be super friendly.

The same thing applies to events, parties, conferences, etc. where we're all there for the same reason, perhaps to celebrate the same person. There's a connection, a reason, a purpose and, yet, even then it takes a lot for us to muster up enough energy to greet one another.

I have an idea for you. Wouldn't it be great if you chose warm and fuzzy t-shirt sayings such as: *It's all about love, Hello, Beautiful, We're all fabulous, Hello,* and every time you put on that t-shirt, you had to become that message? You would need to shift your mindset and 'feel' the words that were written.

Case-in-point--I have a great t-shirt that I love. It says *Compassion* on it. That's it. Just Compassion. I noticed a few times when I wore it that I was anything but compassionate. Maybe I was in a grumpy mood. I just knew that I wasn't being or feeling compassionate. The next time I wore that shirt I made a decision that I was going to embody the message. And I did. My day dramatically shifted. I embodied compassion. I could feel compassion in my bones. It was an incredibly soul-lifting experience when I made the decision to BE my saying on my shirt. It's a good mood lifter.

Here's what I'm suggesting — a challenge. Select 7 t-shirts that have great sayings on them, positive sayings that resonate with you. The whole point is to have uplifting messages. Wear a different one each day for a week. If you have to be in corporate attire, you may be able to get away with a t-shirt under a blazer. The whole point is that you need to 'feel' the message. If this proves to be a no-go, then start this 7-day challenge when you know you can wear the shirts. Or, start when you're on holiday. It doesn't matter. If 7 days is tough, then do it for 2 days on the weekend. I encourage you to just try it.

Notice how you start to shift your mindset when you start to connect with your message. Think of it as being *one with your shirt.* Your message will come out loud and clear. Watch how your disposition changes. Watch how you engage with others. Watch how people respond to your message on your shirt.

The worst is when someone is wearing a shirt that says *Be the Love,* and he or she is anything but love. Who we are, how we act in the world, how we connect with others, and what we bring to the world is our choice. Choose to be the positive messages that you need to convey.

In this day and age, it's needed.

## To Be Your Truth:

Get started. Select some t-shirts with positive messaging and 'be one with your shirt.' Embody your shirt and its message. Have fun!

Amy Goldberg

# What Can You Expect?

I guarantee you that if you continue down the same path that you're going, expect the same results. If you're happy with that path, great. If, however, it's the path of least resistance, then rethink your path. If you're not thrilled with where you are in your life, then you need to take action. Stop looking around and start soul searching. Yes. Search your soul, you're very being for the answers. They are there. If you haven't found that 'thing' that is uniquely yours, that 'thing' that excites you, gives you energy, then you're not finished exploring yet.

**What can you expect?** In a time of instant gratification and celebrity status seekers, you need to know that overnight success takes no less than 5 years and for most 12+ years. Having said that, you better be enjoying the process. If you're driving toward the end goal and dreading the process to get there, guess what? It's not your 'thing.' It's just not.

Of course, you're going to have some powerful wins and some ego-testing blows during your journey. It's all about learning and growing. Sometimes the fruits of your labor come in a way that's so subtle that your success just sneaks up on you. That's how blurred the lines are when you've found your 'thing.' You can also expect to be tested constantly by those that have opinions and by your doubting yourself. And it will happen.

If you're not asking for someone's opinion or seeking advice, then put blinders on and get really focused on your intent, the 'thing' that you found for yourself. Don't let others bring you down. They may sound like the voice of reason, and, yet, they have no idea. They're not in your shoes. Sure, people can offer their experiences and wisdom, and, yet, remember, it's from their perspective--not yours.

You owe it to yourself, your happiness, your life to follow what it is that has you leaping out of bed. Just know that you have control over your expectations, your focus, your intention, and yourself. These are all choices you can make. It's in your hands.

Now, go get it.

## To Be Your Truth:

This comes back to trusting yourself. What are you willing to do to change your life? You can expect the same if you're doing the same. If you want to make a change, then you're going to have to shift or pivot.

Amy Goldberg

# Where Do We Go from Here?

As you start to become more aware of who you are (let me rephrase that)-- as you start to discover more about yourself, you start to recognize that you've had the ability to create what you wanted all along. The only person holding you back is yourself. I'm not completely convinced that you know this. Sure, you get excited and pumped up every time you hear a motivational talk, when you hear someone who inspires you. And, yet, left to your own devices, do you tend to fall back into your own patterns, your own limiting beliefs?

*Why is that?* I believe that we learn how to be disciplined when we have found what it is that excites us or brings us joy. When we have found that 'thing' that has us wanting to move into action, then we have found what will keep our attention. You can't take this lightly. It's a BIG deal when you finally know what it is that puts a smile on your face.

Too often we settle. You may not know that you should be following your heart and happiness. More often than not, you may feel as though your 'work' should be tied to the other obligations in your life. This could be coming from your parents, or it could be perceived responsibilities. I say "perceived" because each and every one of us has a choice in life. We may not feel as if we do, and, yet, we do.

I've heard people say, *I have no choice. I have to take care of* .... Whatever it may be, we all have a choice. You may be choosing the wrong thing for yourself. How do you know when it's the wrong choice? You know when you feel trapped, when you feel there's no way out, when you're stuck, when you're depressed and in despair. All of these are lousy feelings.

When you ask yourself *Where do I go from here?* start to explore where you currently are in your life. Take a look at where you are and what you're doing. Are you satisfied? Are you energized? Are you staying curious? Do you feel joy?

I love the excerpt in Chelsea Handler's book "Life Will Be The Death Of Me," when she says, *Go after happiness like it is the only thing you can take with you when you die.* Imagine if you took that idea and put it into reality. I bet you'd make very different decisions in your life. My feeling is that you'd quickly steer away from wanting 'stuff' or accumulating 'stuff.' Any drama in your life would diminish and/or hopefully disappear, and you'd quickly start to recognize what brings you joy and what doesn't. Wow imagine if you lived your life like this. My sense is you'd also start to experience more-- a lot more.

The thing that really gets me is that you already know this to be true. Or, at the very least, you have a feeling that this kind of life would be far more satisfying. Then why is it so difficult to embody it, to embrace it, to grab a hold of it, and just GO? Apart from fear ... one word-- EGO (all caps). Hard stop. No need to even explain ... and, yet, I will.

I've always admired the teachings of Eckart Tolle, a spiritual leader. A guy who, at a very early age, struggled. He was lost. He suffered from a deep depression. It wasn't until he lived on the streets for a year that he came to a profound understanding of what life was all about. The good news is that you don't need to go through what Eckart did to understand yourself better. As Glenda the good witch in "The Wizard of Oz" tells Dorothy, *You've had the power all along.* And you do.

Why don't you use it? What stops you? Simple answer--you do.

In my earlier years, I had a much gentler approach when it came to motivating others to take action. I took a 'benefit of the doubt' point of view in which I gave people a break when I heard lots of excuses as to why they weren't doing something – especially when I knew they really wanted it. Today, however, I'm less 'forgiving' because I better understand that you are not helping yourself. You are doing yourself a disservice, and I refuse to play into it anymore. I can quickly assess within the first 30 minutes of a conversation if the person/team I'm working with is/are ready to take action.

Think about it. There are already external struggles, challenges, and roadblocks that you may be battling. My job is to take them down, and, yet, not if you're going to put them back up again. You do this single-headedly, on your own. It makes no sense. It's like the addict that is just not quite ready to quit. Yes, it takes time. I'm the last line of defense when it comes to helping people move to the next level of their lives. My approach, or, at least I've been told, is a combination of being enthusiastic, motivating, and inspiring, all the while being tough. I will not let you off the hook.

So, where do you go from here? Consider this ...This is your one life. I'm going to say that again. This is your ONE life or, at least, the one that you remember. You owe it to yourself to make it the best life possible. This means being the kind of person that wholeheartedly embraces life. I can say for sure that a very small proportion of people lead this kind of life. We so desperately want to be seen and, yet, we're going about it in the wrong way. It's not about keeping up with the Kardashians or any other family that's in the spotlight. It's about opening your heart and soul to yourself and others. It really is all about love. I'm not sure if this really and soulfully means anything to anybody. It has become a word, even a brand, rather than a feeling. In case you need a reminder:

Definition

**Love**

An intense feeling of deep affection.

An unselfish loyal and benevolent concern for the good of another.

As you start to observe more closely your behavior and actions, start to rethink and/or start to shift your mindset around how you're leading your life. Make conscious choices rather than keeping the status quo. One way to do this is to schedule out for the year what you want to accomplish. Search out the kinds of experiences that you want to have and book them. Enter them into your calendar. Maybe you need to train, study, or apply for something. You'll need to take some kind of action toward whatever it is that you want to accomplish or experience. Do it! Start taking action toward where you go from here.

## To Be Your Truth:

Start to design your life. Take the same amount of effort that you do planning other things in your life, i.e., vacations, events, work projects--and start creating your own life. Understand that things may shift, and, yet, you have something that you can dig into and get excited about.

## Wake Up And Think!

Truth: We are born, and then we die.

We know this. I'm not sure if we think about it that often, and, yet, there it is. We don't know when we'll die; we know only that we will, eventually. The goal, however, is to lead as long and as healthy a life as we can. You have more control over our health and well-being then we know. Society, however, tends to favor youth, and, therefore, what happens is it may unintentionally (although I feel it's intentional) be dismissing a growing population of those getting older. What I mean by dismiss is more like make 'invisible.'

From a personal perspective, this became most evident to me when my mother was alive. As a general observation, I now see this all the time. My eyes are wide open. What is it that I'm seeing? My mother was a smart and articulate woman. When she moved into her late 80's, she became a lot slower physically and, yet, was still sharp as a tack. She knew what she wanted and what she didn't. When it was time for my mother to sell her home, she and I met with a few realtors. My mother was pretty set on one particular person, and, yet, she wanted to make sure it was the right fit. So, she met with other realtors.

What I observed every time we would meet with someone was that the questions would be directed to me. It was if my mother were invisible. What I did as a way of guiding the conversation was to look at my mother every single time a realtor would ask 'me' a question. I wouldn't answer it. My mother, as well, saw that the person was not directing the questions to her. She was not happy about it. To her credit, my mother eventually had to say, *You know, I'm the one selling my home. Please direct questions to me.* I uttered under my breath; *Yes!* because I was seconds away from saying something myself. However, I didn't want to embarrass my mother. I also knew that she'd handle it. And she did.

What I gleaned from these interactions was that there wasn't any communication with my mother. People would make a snap judgement based on my mother's fragility. Not cool. No one needs to be dismissed because of a perceived fragility. Living your life is challenging enough without adding the effects of ageism to the list. Being your truth means having compassion and understanding for all human beings.

I'm not naïve. I get it. A majority of people will never live their truth. They will struggle. They will screw people over or, worse, cause bodily harm. In a perfect world in which everyone was living their truth, this book wouldn't need to be written. You wouldn't need self-help or personal development guidance. The reality is we all need help.

## To Be Your Truth:

Become more aware of how you interact with people. Biases are an unfair assessment of another. Don't lead with judgement.

Amy Goldberg

# **Influence, This**

In recent years the word or title of "influencer" has been watered down so much that it now sounds rather trite. So, what is an influencer anyway?

**Definition of an influencer**

*noun*

A person or thing that influences another.

More notably: A person with the ability to influence potential buyers of a product or service by promoting or recommending the items on social media.

A quick backgrounder: the word *influencer* has been used since the mid-1600s, when it was used broadly to refer to someone or something with the power to alter the beliefs of individuals and, as a result, impact the course of events. Today, however, there are a number of variations on the influencer theme, such as: *thought leaders, thinkfluencers, micro-influencers,* and *nano-influencers.*

Does this sound to you like a bunch of egocentric mumbo-jumbo created by marketers? Don't we all have the ability to influence others at some point or another? Why do we have to give it a title or call it a job? Quite ironically, it's not even that others are calling people influencers. It's the perceived influencer that has given himself or herself that moniker.

So, why do I find the whole thing rather ridiculous? Because once again we're looking either to create something out of thin air hoping with little effort that something magical will happen or we're looking to others rather than to ourselves to find the answers.

So often people say, *Find someone who inspires you and is doing what you want to be doing and copy THAT.* Forget that your personality, background, experiences, values, skills, etc. could be so misaligned that it actually sets you back rather than propels you forward. Rather than following the masses, create, test, and test again your own theory, sweet spot, and energy around what it is that sparks you. When you find that for yourself, then others will tap into what you're doing--not from an "influencer" standpoint, but rather from a collaborative, supportive, community building aspect to it.

OK, so back to influencers. The bottom line is that influencers want to sell you stuff. Apart from marketing themselves, they are marketing "stuff." What happens is we start to distrust what it is that they're selling. Typically, when one is paid to sell, then that person causes uncertainty about the validity of what he or she is saying. Do we really believe that it's the BEST thing ever? It very rarely, if ever, is. In fact, it kind of backfires. Think about it, **brands say** *partnering with influencers is a great way to sell because their audience puts a lot of* *trust in them and their expertise*. This is ridiculous. Why should you trust people who are getting paid to say what they say? Their word means nothing.

The thing is you need to form your own opinion by gathering information from various sources. There is no one person, no one way of thinking, no gospel, for that matter, that's the magic bullet. It's a matter of discovering as much of the truth as you can and then making an informed decision that works for you.

*I say, influence what you can control – and that's yourself.*

## To Be Your Truth:

Be your own 'influencer.' Trust that you know what want and need. Trust that you will find the answers for yourself.

## You Are How You Act

Think about it. How you act is how you are. Act as if you already have what you want. Watch what happens. If you want to be in love, then act as if you're already in love. If you want to succeed in something, act as if you've already succeeded. You will start to do things differently. Observe the actions that you take.

*Why am I telling you this?* Typically, we rely on and look to others to show us how we should act. Maybe it started when we were little and our parents (guardian) directed us on how we should act, behave, and, basically, be in this world. At least, this was true at the beginning when we were too young to think for ourselves. I believe we may have kept some of these traits. And, perhaps, this influenced how we look to others before we look to ourselves.

I touched on this example earlier in the book, and, yet, it's worth repeating. Have you ever walked into a room, looked around, and connected with people who smiled at you and you smiled back? You were getting a sense of the room, the vibe, and the energy of others. You were setting yourself up for a good experience.

In an exact same scenario, however, you walked into the room, looked around, and, yet, you were not feeling great about yourself. You had rushed to get there; you had tried on 10 outfits before settling on something that didn't fit well. You got a sense of the room, the vibe, the energy and yet it didn't feel quite right. People looked over at you, and you looked back and thought, *What are you looking at?* Your smile was nowhere to be seen. You had now set the tone for a 'different' kind of experience.

Here lies the truth. How you show up and how you act in every single situation, scenario, experience set the tone for everything that you do-- for the choices that you make; the actions that you take (or don't take); and your all-round disposition. There's a lot going on in that blink of an eye! *So why not make the best of it?*

Show up like an athlete. Train your brain and body for action. Visualize the outcome that you want. *Act as if.* It's incredible how 3 little words put together can have such an astounding outcome IF you *Act as if* you want it.

We get so wrapped up into thinking that we're not good enough, when, in fact, we're probably not giving ourselves a fighting chance. We're relying on old tapes that are playing on repeat in our minds. Press **STOP**. And **DO NOT PRESS PLAY** unless you're ready for real play to play an active and positive role in your life, to act in a way that resembles a kind, grateful, energetic, positive, action-oriented human being that is ready to thrive rather than just survive. Your actions start with you. It's not easy when you've conditioned yourself not to show up in a way that will best serve your positive self.

Start acting in the way you want to be treated. Start acting as if you are the most incredible human being on this planet. Watch what happens. You'll start to see a shift. This shift will not only serve you for the better, it will act as a catalyst where others will follow this stream of positive consciousness. I kid you not.

*It's not Woo Woo, It's Wow!*

## To Be Your Truth:

Start practicing until it becomes a natural part of you. Start *'acting as if ...'*

Amy Goldberg

# Changing Perception

*Common sense is not so common.*

## - Voltaire

This book wouldn't be reflective of who I am without talking about your health. -- more from the perspective of your mindset. One thing I know is that you have been hardwired in some way or another since birth because of health scares, conflicting and contradicting information, being misguided, marketing scams-- you name it. You constantly need to adjust and change your habits because some decisions that you're making may not be best for you.

If you choose not to adopt new habits, you inevitably resort to old ones. Case-in-point-- albeit dramatic-- you had a health scare; all the symptoms pointed to a stroke - pain, paralysis, disorientation, weakness, nausea, sweats, fear--you are rushed to the hospital. A series of tests are taken. There is one appointment after another. Tests finally show that you are fine; it was only a warning to take better care of yourself. So, you begin to eat well, exercise, drop weight, become less depressed, your strength is coming back, and you start to feel better.

But here's the thing: a few months pass, and you are heard saying, *Tonight, we're going to the Legion to have fish and chips.* It took just a couple of months to go back to old and true habits. Is it because you begin to feel better and you lose the memory of ever feeling the pain of illness? Quite possibly, yes. Another reason is because it's very difficult to de-program you from old habits and re-program yourself for better ones.

It takes the desire to want to change, the willpower to make the change lasting, and a plan to ensure that you make it happen. We all have it in us. Our life is based on change and choices. What choices are you now thinking about in order to live a healthier and happier life? The answers are there. It just depends upon on how badly you want it.

Changing perception takes consistency. Any kind of change requires you to repeat the behavior until it becomes a habit. An example of this is brushing your teeth, a simple yet effective example of something that you 'just do.' Begin to adopt habits that will help you to become a stronger, healthier, happier, and more energetic you. Feeling better about yourself is empowering. You have everything that you need to get started. Don't be afraid to ask for help.

## To Be Your Truth:

Start to adopt new healthy habits. Habits that will make you feel stronger. The easiest way to do this is to replace an old unhealthy habit with a new healthy habit. Rather than giving up something, you're replacing. It works!

Amy Goldberg

# Guilt Works, Only Temporarily

A friend of mine messaged me saying that today she scheduled a call with a fellow speaker from a summit where they both were. My friend said, *Is it me, or do people think I'm an easy mark for a sale?* She went on to say that she felt so pressured to sign up and pay a ridiculous monthly fee for that person to help her get speaking gigs. After my friend said no, the person completely made her feel like shit. My friend concluded by saying that she *gets that it's a sales tactic, and, yet, wow!*

There are so many things wrong with this scenario that I'm not sure where to begin. The truth is no one actually can make you feel a certain way. It's on you. And, yet, here we have a fellow speaker pressuring a fellow speaker. I know that when I meet other speakers at events, I'm excited to get to know them. What happens in a lot of cases, however, is that some are overly eager to cut to the chase. They want to know all about you, and then, BAM, they go in for the kill. It goes like this: *Let's set up a call or go for coffee.* I must admit that I get sucked into meeting up or having that call in the hope that it's not a sales pitch. The funny thing is that I instinctively know whether the person is going to pitch me or not. I think I agree to a follow-up just to prove myself wrong. Nope. It never happens. And, of course, I am always disappointed.

In the short run, the person thinks the playbook that he or she is following is kosher. They feel the steps they are following are perfectly fine. Afterall, we're all selling something, right? Wrong. Wrong tactic. Why? -- because it's a tactic. We are in such a hurry to get 'the sale' that we completely sabotage any chance of building trust, building fruitful relationships, being authentic and credible. We burn bridges so fast that we limit the direction that we can take. You certainly can't back track. We have burned the bridge behind us.

You need to decide what it is that you're hoping to attain. If you're leading with the end in mind that is making a sale, it rarely works unless the person already knows what he or she wants, and, even then, you should not approach any sort of engagement or interaction with a pitch. We can smell it a mile away.

Why do we do this? We're certainly not leading with our truth. This can't be matching how our soul wants to speak? This is where, at the end of the day, we start to question our behavior. This questioning period can manifest itself through illness, arguments, loneliness, unhappiness, weight gain, clumsiness. There are a number of ways by which misalignment can transpire. Most of the time we don't equate our actions with other things that are going on in our lives. It may not occur to us to take a deeper look into ourselves to see what's really going on.

This is why when something happens to us that is catastrophic, we start to pivot. We start to open our eyes to a different reality. This is driven by fear. However, if you can get past the fear and into your truth, this is where the magic happens. I believe this is probably the only time when we don't feel guilty, when we press pause on ourselves and stop to see our own mortality.

Isn't it interesting how our feelings of guilt quickly diminish? It's a mindset. It's a time to reflect on what's really going on. I always say that if someone is bold enough to push you into a corner, get out of there. Your truth will set you free. Trust yourself.

Guilt reminds you that you're not in tune with who you truly are. When you feel guilt, you know something is up. You're not in balance with your truth. Take a look at the next time guilt triggers you. See what's going on within you. You'd be surprised at what you notice. Remember guilt is just a symptom of something else. And others will prey on that. Stop them in their tracks. Speak your truth.

## To Be Your Truth:

When you know your truth, you will speak your truth. Every time you feel a pang of guilt, check in with yourself. Ask yourself, *Why am I feeling guilty?* You'll find the answer you need.

## What's Really Going On?

What's really going on in this world? I'm finding more and more that people are a lot less polite and a lot more entitled? When did this happen? I feel as if I closed my eyes for a moment and things changed on a dime. Interestingly, in a world where you see more social media posts around gratitude, meditation, self-love, compassion, and a greater drive for emotional well-being, we seem to have interpreted all of this in a more self-absorbed manner. Why?

The truth is I'm baffled. Maybe it's because social media has created an unleashed beast where the 'get rich quick' mentality is on the rise. Everything looks so much easier than one realizes. When, in actual fact, that 'overnight success,'--well, you know how long it takes--years. And, yet, most people, unless they've been through it, have no idea.

I've been asked to speak at a number of events for 'creatives and entrepreneurs' where the most asked question is: *How do I fast-track what I want to do?* This means how do I go from 0-120mph to ramp up my business with as little effort as possible. My response is,

*Try it your way. Miss steps, create half-assed material, pitch what you think you're offering ...."* IF, that doesn't work, then I'm suggesting that you *Take a step back and then propel forward. Define what it is you want to achieve, and then walk it back from there.* It's called 'reverse engineering,' and, yet, that term is so overused that I didn't want to be a lemming. There you go!

We all deserve to lead the best possible lives. Why there is so much struggle and inequality in this world is incredibly disheartening. The fact that a lot of people wake up every day and just try and make ends meet is no way to lead a life. What's the alternative? -- a different way of thinking for all of us, a way in which no one would feel alone, lonely, isolated, and left to their own understanding of their circumstances, as they currently are.

When you're 'in it,' when you can't see the forest for the trees, you have no idea what your options are. This is when you need the most help. You need to hear that you do, in fact, have options. That you do, in fact, have people around you that care. If I'm stating this, then there better be that community at the other end of that lifeline. Is there? I'm asking you.

Do you feel that everyone deserves a fulfilling life free from hardship and struggle? If so, are you willing to be the one that leads with a smile and demonstrates that you care. I'm not talking about a handout; I'm talking about a hand up, a chance for someone to know that if he or she needed support, you'd bring your positivity, your inspiring self, and your kindness. You see, it takes each and every single one of us to do this. What is required is for us to pause when we find ourselves too much into ourselves to worry about anyone else. What we need to consider is that no one stands alone when he or she seeks for what is needed and wanted. Everyone has someone to help get them there.

Wouldn't it be great if you could do that for someone else? What it really takes is acknowledging others, their circumstances, and the shoes they walk in. It's not easy. We're so busy trying to get ahead of the curve ball ourselves, let alone having time to try and guide others. But, the biggest reward in life is to help others.

## To Be Your Truth:

Take your time. You will get there. If you expect things to happen right away, then you're setting yourself up for a lot of disappointment. When you begin to show others that you're there to support them (in your authentic way), they will want to support you. Begin with kindness.

Amy Goldberg

## I'll Do It Later

Have you ever found yourself continually looking to join, attend, read, consume as much self-help information as you can and then find that you're no further ahead than when you first started? When this happens, it starts to become something of a procrastination tactic. You may not be aware that you're stalling or resisting whatever it is that's holding you back. You may not want to face it head on, and, yet, I'm here to tell you that it's time. It's time to get out of your own way and start taking action. Resistance is the one thing that holds you back from ever realizing your aspirations, dreams, goals, whatever it is that you want to attain.

You, actually, may not have a clue as to where to start or how to get there, and, yet, I'm here to say start anyway. Try things. Experience things. If you don't take some kind of action, you will start to feel less of yourself. You will begin to feel defeated, diminished, and discouraged. And, yet, in reality, you can't actually have any of these feelings IF you haven't yet tried. You actually need to start doing something.

Funny how that happens. The feeling you may be facing right now is the feeling of being 'numb'-- numb to the fact that you may feel lost or stuck. You may feel this way because you're dragging yourself around without a direction, with no sense of purpose or passion. This I like to call that thing that excites you, that gives you energy.

Right now, you may be feeling as if you're just trying to get through the day. And yet let's think about that. 'Getting through the day'-- that can't be good. If you're finding that day after day you're saying, *When this is over, done, completed .... THEN I can ....* or you're saying, *Only if ....* then you need to rethink what you're doing. You're always hoping for something to change or to be over with in order for you to be happier. It won't happen. There will always be something else--always.

I hear this often from people of all backgrounds, experiences, education, socio-economic conditions--you name it. What is our fascination with speeding up time to get to less time? What about right now? That's all we have. What about looking into why you feel what you're doing

now needs to be *gotten over with.* If you're feeling that way, then you need to consider what's going on. Are you trying to lead someone else's life and that's why you hope it's over with soon? Are you working at something that makes you miserable, and you want to get it done as fast as possible so that you can …. You can what? -- go on to the next thing that you need to get over with? This cycle does not go away.

You will be repeating this behavior until you break the cycle, until you decide to shift your mindset or pivot. You have a choice. You have many choices. Pick one. Pick the one that never has you saying ever again, *I just need to get over, or do this, before I ....* Once you're able to do this, watch what happens. You no longer will be living for the weekends or making decisions for anyone other than yourself. You will be leading your life by your truth. No one else needs to apply. I promise you this will be liberating. This could be a turning point for you. This could mean that you are finally going to embrace your truth.

## To Be Your Truth:

Shift your mindset. Pick one thing that does not have you wanting you to *get it over with.*

Begin there.

## As You Start To Walk On The Way

*As you start to walk on the way, the way appears.– Rumi*

I use this quote a lot. It's by Rumi, a scholar, poet, spiritual thinker, and philosopher. I refer to it when I do presentations, public speaking. It's even on my website. It's about time I wrote about why it is that I like this quote so much. Why it resonates with me and will, hopefully, with you too.

*Let's break it down.*

***As you start to walk ....*** This quote requires you to take *action*, some kind of action, action even in the face of self-doubt, fear, and one's limiting beliefs. It's having trust in yourself to follow your bliss or what brings you joy – even if you're not entirely sure what that is.

***... on the way ...*** It also creates some kind of awareness. When you start to take notice that you're following a certain path, then things will happen. Something WILL happen.

*... the way appears.* This is where you need to trust, have faith, follow your gut instinct. It could be karma. Whatever it is for you, it requires you to understand that as you start to notice your life, notice where you're walking (metaphorically speaking), trying and experiencing new things, often the "way" opens up for you. It appears from the sheer fact that you're taking notice. You're exploring further-- expanding your horizons.

Additional thinking has us saying that *Often, I have been afraid to walk the way because I lacked the self-determination and the self-power go forward. My beliefs, my conditioning, and my doubts got the better of me, and I stopped short; I quit; I doubted; I procrastinated; I made excuses; I let go of things before they could bloom into a great possibility. Rumi advises you to go ahead and walk on your journey. Even though you may doubt yourself, stay firm in your self-affirmation. Make a decision and move forward*--an excerpt from the blog Launch My Genius by Harish.

Clinical psychologist, Tari Mack, writes, As *you walk in the direction toward which you feel pulled, doors will continue to open. Follow your joy. Follow your heart. Follow your intuition. Keep gently scooting fear to the side; keep gently shushing it. Yes, fear, I know you're there. And that's okay. Just keep going. As you walk on the way, the way appears. Keep walking.*

All this reinforces the thinking that we tend to get in our own way. Fear stops us in our tracks. Imagine if you simply acknowledged the fear, understood that it does serve you well in times when you *really* need it. However, in the case where you're moving from being comfortable to uncomfortable, know that fear does not serve you. It blocks you. Walk past it. Break through it. Move into action. Trust that *As You Start To Walk On The Way, The Way Appears.*

## To Be Your Truth:

Keep going. Keep asking yourself, *What's holding me back? Why am I resisting?* It's time to trust your path, your journey. Your instincts and intuition will kick in when you let go of your fear.

Amy Goldberg

# You Are One Decision Away From Changing Your Life

The truth is intellectually we understand that we are one decision away from changing our lives. However, emotionally, that's a whole other story. We're not the greatest at taking in this kind of information and then turning it into action. We tend to make a lot of excuses. It helps to justify why we're not doing something. For some reason, we feel we need to be superhuman with rock solid will power if we want to make any real change in our life.

To cite a few examples: Why do we treat and feed our bodies as if they were toxic dumping grounds and then hope for super energy all day long? Why do we fall into the same patterns that sabotage our efforts to find joy in our lives? Why do we work in roles that make us miserable? Why do we feed into negativity causing us undue stress and anxiety? We must know that all of these things are toxic. Don't we?

To change the way we live is to make other choices. It takes clicking a switch in our brain that doesn't have us repeating the same destructive habits and patterns. But, how do we do this? How do we pivot? One person who feels she has the answer is Mel Robbins, a motivational speaker turned TV show host. She helps people lead happier lives. She first became known when she discovered that by counting: 5-4-3-2-1 and then taking action, it worked.

What's her reasoning behind this? It doesn't give us time to 'think.' It doesn't allow us to make excuses because the idea is to count and leap. It does work IF you take action right away. You must respond after counting. Eventually, if you do this all the time, your brain will respond faster. You'll be creating a new pattern that moves you into action. In reality, ANY tool will work IF the trigger has you taking action. What stops us from taking action, however, is that we are so paralyzed by our own complacency, fear, and anxiety that it can become a real struggle to overcome and ignore the easier way out. Why? -- because doing nothing is far easier. *However, this is no way to lead your life. You deserve more. We all do.*

It's human nature to find the easiest way with the least amount of resistance to doing anything. However, when you start to make the decision to change one thing, you will start to change many things. Treat it like a game. Challenge the status quo and shake things up. You probably will have to force yourself for the first little while. After that, it'll become easier. Remember, you don't have a problem if you can solve it. Almost every single problem is solvable. That's comforting.

*How do you start?* Make one decision to change something, now. It doesn't matter what it is. Maybe you have the same evening pattern when after your day, you go home and watch tv. You land on that couch and don't move a muscle. How about breaking that pattern, and, one day a week, you do something else? Join a group, a class, exercise, meet up with a friend, start writing a book you've been wanting to start, work on something that could lead you into a different career direction. It doesn't matter. *Just start.*

Remember, you are one decision away from changing your life. If you want something, start going after it. Declare what you want. Don't, and I mean do not, allow anyone to derail you. You are leading your life. You are not responsible for living someone else's. I'm not going to kid you. It's really tough to make changes in your life, even when you know that it would be great for you. Fear is a powerful emotion. Fear always appears real in your mind. You 'feel' it in your bones. And, yet, I'm here to say that it's time to make fear your friend rather than your foe.

Have you ever watched the Seinfeld episode in which the character George decides that if everything he's doing now isn't working in his life, he's going to do the opposite? Every time he makes a decision, he quickly thinks about it, and then does the complete opposite. It was as simple as seeing a woman smiling at him, and if he would typically not reciprocate due to being terrified that he'd be rejected, he decides to approach her. They strike up a fabulous conversation which leads to a date. I love that. He mustered up the courage to respond differently in his life. It paid off. And, hey, it may not pay off every time for you, and, yet, the idea is that you're taking action. You're starting to build up your confidence in a way that perhaps you hadn't before. That's where the real magic happens.

In the past, I would hold myself back from sending letters and/or calling people for fear that I would get a lousy response or, worse, no response at all. Then I thought so what. If I don't do anything, then I'm absolutely not going to get a response. It's always worth it-- always.

When you find yourself daydreaming, try and capture what it is that you're dreaming about. Write it down. Start to pull together what it is that keeps capturing your attention. This is a clue to what it is that you really want to move into or what it is that you may be lacking in your current reality. Either way, pay attention. At any time, you do have the choice to choose any direction you want to go in as well as where you don't want to be going. It starts to happen when you start deciding that you're going to move into action.

*What's stopping you? If it's you, then go around yourself.*

Amy Goldberg

## To Be Your Truth:

Make one decision to change something-- now. If you're feeling any kind of resistance within yourself, walk past it. Do it anyway. Try. See what happens.

## The Definition Of You

I don't know if you have ever found yourself labeling someone within the context of what they do? Case in point: I'm going to reference the show Seinfeld again. If you've ever watched it, you may have noticed that the characters refer to people with titles. *Hey, there's the photocopier guy. That's the waitress, teller, car rental person.* I've actually found myself referring to people in that same manner when best describing and/or remembering someone. At the gym, for example, I had a bad habit of referring to people by *Muscle Dave, Dentist Dave (so as not to confuse the two), Bond girl (because she has a cool name and looks like a Bond girl).* You get where I'm going with this? It occurred to me, however, just how narrow-minded that really was.

One thing that I love to do is teach spin classes. It's not my occupation. It's part of the many things that I do. I've noticed that when people introduce me (if they know me as an instructor) will say, *This is Amy. She teaches spin classes.* And, presto, I'm now defined within the limits of this activity. And that does not serve me well. In fact, if we don't learn to discover the many dimensions of a person, then we're missing out on learning more about one another. It's incredibly frustrating to be on the receiving end of this, and, therefore, I have since stopped referring to people in this manner.

Amy Goldberg

We now find it necessary to 'brand' ourselves, to create a nice neat package of ourselves. When we do, it seems to be saying, *Ohhh THAT'S who I am.* Hey, listen, I've found myself doing the exact same thing. It wasn't that long ago that I, too, needed help to discover *who I am* within the context of the work that I was doing. I reached out for help. There is incredible comfort in clearly defining what it is that we DO. However, let's be clear, this is Not to be confused with needing to brand *who you are as* a person.

I don't think we should have to rhyme off who we are to others. As I've mentioned before, we're different every day. Our essence is the same, and yet we are constantly gaining new perspective as we grow. That's what's so cool about us! We can be whoever we want to be. The definition of you as defined by others will always be limiting just as I'm labelled as a spin

instructor within one aspect of the context of someone's knowing me. Apart from this coming from a place of ego because, let's face it, it is. The other side of the coin is to try to make others evolve to a place where they should be more open and interested to learn more about another person.

You see, as much as this is ego, it's also about curiosity. If you tap into your curiosity, then you will find that you won't label people. You'll want to learn and know more. That's what curiosity does. This is why we tend to lead limiting lives. We're not tapping into our curiosity enough to want to be and do more. This is part of developing and evolving into yourself. This is where you have to push fear aside and take a leap of faith within yourself. To know that if you try, you will evolve. This is profound.

The next time someone wants to define you, step in from a place of curiosity rather than ego. For example, my reply to someone who introduces me as a spin instructor would be, *Yes! Teaching spin classes first thing in the morning really opens up my energy & creativity to be a better writer--* or international inspirational speaker, producer, well-being entrepreneur, business strategist, and coach …. You get my drift? Of course, words help shape what we do and who we are, and, yet, they should not define us.

Bottom line: Evolve into yourself. Discover more.

## To Be Your Truth:

Get curious. Stop yourself from labelling people. Find out more about the person by listening.

Amy Goldberg

# The Path of Least Resistance

I read the book *The War of Art* by Steven Pressfield in which he talks about Resistance being an enemy to everything that we seek. He goes on to create a **Resistance Greatest Hits** – which I'd like to share with you in case you haven't read his book. Pressfield writes: *The following is in no particular order. These are the activities that most <u>commonly elicit Resistance</u>:*

- *The pursuit of any calling in writing, painting, music, film, dance, or any creative art, however marginal or unconventional*
- *The launching of any entrepreneurial venture or enterprise, for profit or otherwise*
- *Any diet or health regimen*
- *Any program of spiritual advancement*
- *Any activity whose aim is tighter abdominals*
- *Any course or program designed to overcome an unwholesome habit or addiction*
- *Education of every kind*

Be Your Truth

- *Any act of political, moral, or ethical courage, including the decision to change for the better some unworthy pattern of thought or conduct in ourselves*
- *The undertaking of any enterprise or endeavor whose aim is to help others*
- *Any act that entails commitment of the heart, the decision to get married, to have a child, to weather a rocky patch in a relationship*
- *The taking of any principled stand in the face of adversity*

Pressfield continues to say, *In other words, any act that rejects immediate gratification in favor of long-term growth, health, or integrity or, expressed in another way, any act that derives from our higher nature instead of our lower--any of these will elicit Resistance.* Not only is this enlightening, he has a great sense of humor about it all. What he's getting at is that Resistance is a negative force that keeps us from doing our work. And if we take Resistance at its word, we deserve everything we get. Resistance is always lying to us and always full of hot air.

It's actually very helpful to understand better what's holding us back. It doesn't make it any easier, however. What it does do is have you recognize that Resistance is not to be trusted. It is your mortal enemy. Pressfield goes on to say that the *Rule of Thumb: The more important a call or action is to our soul's evolution, the more Resistance we will feel toward pursuing it.* Now THAT'S good to know. He's basically saying that if you feel Resistance toward something you know to be true … do it anyway.

Resistance by definition is self-sabotage. Master our fear of Resistance and we conquer Resistance. The only person fueling this fear is you. So, when I'm constantly writing about, *It Starts With You and What's Holding You Back?* -- guess what? It's Resistance...and fear and …. Life is a struggle. No human being is immune to Resistance-- no one. What's sad is if you give into Resistance and leave this world without giving it all that you've got. You'd think that we would wake up to the fact that we truly have nothing to lose if we just did the work, if we simply did what needed to be done, if we trusted ourselves enough to muffle the noise.

I wonder how many times you'd need to do this before it would go away completely. OK, reality check – Resistance is NEVER going away. You just need to manage it in a way in which you're not drawn to give it any attention. This way you can go on with your life in a way that best serves you. *I'm all for that!*

## To Be Your Truth:

Resistance does not serve you. Start to take notice. Pay attention to when you resist doing something.

Amy Goldberg

## Trust Your Truth

*I have been a seeker and I still am, but I stopped asking the books and the stars. I started listening to the teachings of my Soul.* – Rumi

My quest has been about observing and understanding human behavior. Gathering information through the perspective of others, books, courses, philosophers, travel. Although helpful, the reality is that it didn't quite have me finding 'me.' These distractions, as I now know, didn't give me the courage to dig deep enough into my soul, even when I knew my truth to be real. I felt that if I did dig deep, it would feel too self-absorbed and egotistical, finding my truth seems self-centered. As a giver, it just felt strange to me. And, yet, I know that simply wasn't true.

Of course, I recognize that this was my way of not having to deal with my feelings. I'm a strong person, a crusader for all things kind and humane, and, yet, I felt as if I were fighting a battle within myself--that battle of disconnectedness, unease, and aloneness. I masked it with my enthusiasm and happy disposition. Interestingly, I've observed that it's the happy-go-lucky people in the world that tend to be uncomfortable sharing their feelings. That <u>was</u> me.

The 'me' that helped others. The me that, if you were going down in a plane crash, would put the oxygen mask on you before myself. Well, we know that's wrong. Ironically, the top of my priority list is to take care of my health and well-being so that I can be more helpful to others. So why would this be any different?

Guess what? If you don't reveal your truth, then you will never get close enough to yourself--which means you will have a tough time being close with others. How could you if you're not close with yourself? When you start to identify and write down your truth, your truth will unfold. Recognize that your fears are what's holding you back and know that fear is not your enemy. It is your accepting relationship to fear that reveals a trusted friend over a foe.

Surrendering to your fear is your intuition revealed. When you embrace fear, you are then one decision away from changing your life. Once this happens, trust will lead you out of fear, and accessing your intuition unlocks the value of your valor. This is where empowerment reveals itself. No longer enslaved to what you were previously afraid of reveals a clear path to (re)claim the life of your dreams. I say it's time to receive. It's time for you. You don't need to feel enclosed or sheltered from your own self. You can rise above and start to Trust Rise. That's powerful.

You can pivot in life as many times as you see fit. Pivoting is just another way of saying *This isn't working for me.* This is not fear or failure. This should not define you. What you're creating is a happier, healthier, more authentic and true self. You shouldn't worry about what others have to say or think about you. You are that person that will determine where you are. You know that your truth is yours and no one else's. This is your journey. One that you get to choose. The truth is that you can make the decision to move in a direction that best serves you. It is not selfish, or ego driven. It's honoring who you are and what speaks to your soul.

Having observed humankind, I believe that we are all searching for that higher ground.

We are all looking for that trust rise. It takes a lifetime for people to be their truth. Many don't achieve this sense of peace or calm. Our morality is wrapped in a warped sense of what we think we should be rather than what we need to be. If you lead with your truth, you wouldn't need any rules. You would instinctively know right from wrong. You would lead with kindness, love, and human compassion. Rather, we become even more confused as we witness the inhumanity to humankind on a daily basis. This is ludicrous.

I'm convinced that the reason we read self-help and personal development books is to have someone else reinforce to us that we're not crazy, that we're not going insane. I find myself saying often, *Is it just me ...?* The noise in your head, your thoughts, your cries--these are shout-outs from your soul to say *You're not listening to me.* You need to feed your soul by first understanding that by trusting your truth, you will have found the way. Trust your truth. It won't lie to you.

**To Be Your Truth is to Trust That You Will Rise. Go Rise.**

## About the Author

Amy Goldberg is the founder of The TRUSTRISE; a movement to elevate people *(individuals, teams, audiences)* to take decisive action toward living their inspired life. She can be found speaking, teaching, consulting, coaching and collaborating for positive result-focused change. People that know her call her a connection specialist. She has the ability to connect you to what would inspire you to rock your life. Amy doesn't entertain the possibility; she IS the possibility. She will show you how to be the possibility. Amy is a powerhouse of energy with an authentic desire to help you lead an inspired life that is disbelief suspended, thinking challenged, and change activated. For more than 25+ years, Amy's been revving at a high vibe. People trust her. Amy delivers results every time because that's who she is -- an unleashed trailblazer.

Email: yes@thetrustrise.com
www.thetrustrise.com

Lightning Source UK Ltd.
Milton Keynes UK
UKHW011309170220
358851UK00003B/1065